ALL THE PRESIDENTS' DATES

THE PRESIDENTIAL TRIVAL BOOK

EVERY AMERICAN HOUSEHOLD SHOULD HAVE

FIFTH EDITION

BY JEAN A. PUPETER

READERS QUILL AGENCY
Where Every Story Finds Its Stage

FIFTH Edition Dedication

The fifth edition is dedicated to my grandson, Caliber Fiebelkorn, who at age 8 exemplifies a curiousity for learning. Special thanks to Dawn Juhl, who typed the first edition and Gary Shaw who edited the first edition, as well as continued thanks and appreciation to Verlene Orr, who has always supported my endeavors.

Fourth Edition Foreword

On November 8, 2016, Americans sat glued to their televisions watching the election returns, "KNOWING" Hillary Clinton would be the victor. Democrats and Republicans alike were convinced the White House would go to American's first woman president. In fact the subtitle of this fourth edition was to be "America's First Woman President."

As the evening wore on, things began to change as states such as Florida, North Carolina, Pennsylvania, and Ohio came in for Donald Trump. When Wisconsin went for Trump late in the evening, many then suspected the election result was not a foregone conclusion. It took until 2:30 am Eastern time to reach the results.

This election was reminiscent of 1948. A famous photo shows Truman holding a Chicago Daily Tribune the morning after the election with a full banner headline that reads "DEWEY DEFEATS TRUMAN'. In fact Truman had garnered 303 electoral votes, but newsprint was behind network radio. In 1948 all major poles, political experts and pundits predicted a Dewey win. A book by Joe Garner, "WE INTERRUPT THIS BROADCAST", states, "By 1952, more sophisticated polling techniques had begun to remove the possibility of such surprises from presidential elections.…" In 2016 pundits tried desperately to figure out why the poles were so inaccurate. The election had followed a cantankerous campaign on both sides with horrible insults being hurled. Nation wide protests followed the election. On December 19, 2016, Electoral College votes were held amid further demonstrations at many State capitals.

Hillary Clinton had won the popular vote, as had Al Gore in 2000 and Grover Cleveland in 1888. However, the Electoral votes went for Donald Trump, George W. Bush and Benjamin Harrison respectively. Thus Donald J. Trump became America's 45th president.

TABLE OF CONTENTS

CHAPTER 1

MR. PRESIDENT, WIDOWER

The term, "Mr. President, Widower", has been used 19 times in U.S. history. Seventeen presidents became widowers at the death of their wives, five of whom remarried: Tyler, Fillmore, Benjamin Harrison, Theodore Roosevelt, and Wilson. The other eleven did not. Five president's wives died before they became first ladies. The five were Martha Jefferson, Rachel Jackson, Hannah Van Buren, Ellen Arthur and Alice Roosevelt. Three first ladies died while their husbands were in office: Letitia Tyler, Caroline Harrison, and Lou Wilson. The other nine first ladies predeceased their husbands after his presidency had been completed.

Abigail Smith Adams was the wife of one president and the mother of another. She was also third cousin to her husband, John Adams. In 1775, Abigail urged her husband to support independence. She believed in the abolition of slavery and in more education for women. Years later she was rated the second most influential first lady, behind Eleanor Roosevelt. John and Abigail Adams retired to Massachusetts after his term as president. They lived there for 17 years until Abigail died at age 73 of typhoid on October 28, 1818. President Adams outlived her for 7 years and wrote of the love and admiration he had for her and his gratitude for her support of his political career. After her death, he lived to see his son, John Quincy Adams, become president.

Martha Wayles Skelton Jefferson was born on October 19, 1748 and was married to Thomas Jefferson for 10 years. Her physical health was weakened by her six pregnancies and she never gained strength after her last child was born in May of 1782. Thomas Jefferson was very devoted to Martha. When she died on September 6, 1782, he wrote in his diary, "My dear wife died this day at 11:45 a.m.". He spent the next three weeks shut in his room, pacing till almost exhausted. Two years later he went to France. It would be 19 years before he became president of the United States and, besides the loss of his wife, four of his children died before he became president. He was the first president to serve as a widower. He had promised Martha on her deathbed that he would never remarry, and he did not. He lived almost 44 years after Martha's death.

Elizabeth Kortwright Monroe died on September 23, 1830, five years after she and James Monroe left the White House. She had been a very aristocratic first lady and was referred to as hauty and a snob by many in the public. James Monroe died a year later, after their brief retirement at Monroe Mansion in Oak Hill, Virginia. Elizabeth Monroe had spent money freely and James Monroe was in serious financial trouble at the time of his death.

Rachel Donelson Robards Jackson was born on June 15, 1767 in Virginia. and moved to Tennessee at age 13. Her abusive first husband, Lewis Robards, caused her to flee to Nashville to get away from continuing harassment. Future president Andrew Jackson took her to Mississippi where, upon receiving word of Mr. Robard's divorce from Rachel, they were married in 1791. They later discovered that Robards had only applied for the divorce and it was not decreed until 1793.

Thus, Andrew Jackson and Rachel remarried on January 17, 1794. A gossipy public repeated a story of Rachel's adultery because her marriage to Andrew Jackson was not legal the first time. During his presidential campaign, she overheard people gossiping about this, as well as her pipe smoking, and she was found weeping hysterically. A few days later she had a heart attack and died on September 22, 1828. She was buried in the inaugural gown she had selected to wear the day her husband would become president. Andrew Jackson was the second widower inaugurated into the executive office. He was heartbroken by Rachel's death and wore a miniature picture of her during his years in the White House. He never remarried.

Hannah Hoes and Martin Van Buren were wed on February 21, 1807. Hannah was a shy, modest, loving and gentle Christian. Hannah died at age 35 of tuberculosis on February 5, 1819, thus making President Van Buren the third widower to be inaugurated president of the United States. Although he never remarried and lived another 43 years, he proposed to Margaret Sylvester, age 40, in 1851. She declined, stating that she wished to remain single, and they remained good friends. Hannah Van Buren was buried in Albany, New York, but Martin Van Buren later had her reburied in Kinderhook.

Letitia Christian Tyler was born on November 12, 1790 and married John Tyler on March 29, 1813, his 23rd birthday. Letitia was crippled by a stroke in 1839 and was an invalid when she became first lady. She lived in seclusion at the White House. Letitia's only appearance at a White House social function was at her daughter Elizabeth's wedding in 1842. She died on September 10, 1842 and was the first first lady to die while her husband was in office. A very depressed husband ordered the White House hung in black for mourning. Tyler then became the first widowed President to remarry while still in office. On June 26, 1844, not two years later, he married Julia Gardiner, age 23. Tyler had had 8 children with Letitia and Julia gave him seven more, the last of which was born when he was 70 years old. Julia survived President Tyler by 27½ years.

Abigail Powers Fillmore was born on March 13, 1798. As a teacher, one of her students was Millard Fillmore. Abigail was also an invalid when she became first lady. She is credited with starting the first library in the White House. In chronically poor health, she attended President Pierce's inauguration as her husband was leaving office and caught a cold, which developed into pneumonia. She died on March 30, 1853, less than a month after her husband left office. The House and Senate adjourned and public offices were closed in respect. President Fillmore lost both his wife and daughter within a year and a half after leaving the White House. The emotional strain of the two deaths weighed heavily on him. However, he became the second widowed president to remarry. On February 10, 1858 he married Carolyn MacIntosh, who survived him.

Jane Appleton Pierce was born on March 12, 1806. As the daughter of the Bowdoin College president, she met Franklin Pierce when he attended that college in Maine. Jane was a petite, frail, shy, religious fanatic. Two of her three sons had died prior to Franklin Pierce being elected president. When she first heard the news that he was nominated, she fainted, because she did not want him in politics. Her only surviving son died two months before the inauguration in a train wreck. She wore black every day in the White House and wrote morbid letters to her deceased son. She died on December 2, 1863 from tuberculosis, leaving Franklin Pierce lonely and depressed. After her death, he drank heavily until his death six years later.

Lucy Webb Hayes was born on August 28, 1831. She became the first college- educated first lady. She had aided the wounded in the Civil War after her marriage to Rutherford B. Hayes. As first lady she was known as "Lemonade Lucy", due to her abhorrence of alcohol. Lucy and Rutherford celebrated their silver wedding anniversary at the White House on December 31, 1877. She was a vigorous opponent of slavery. The Easter Egg Roll on the White House lawn started when Lucy was first lady. After Hayes' presidency, they retired to Ohio happily for eight years. Lucy Hayes died of a stroke on June 25, 1889. She was later known as one of the best-loved first ladies. Four years later in 1893, Rutherford B. Hayes' last words before his death were, "I know that I am going where Lucy is".

Ellen Herndon Arthur, called "Nell", was born on August 30, 1837. Nell was a gifted singer who married Chester Arthur in 1859. She died suddenly from pneumonia on January 12, 1880. Chester Arthur was inconsolable and never really recovered. He became the fourth widower to be inaugurated. He bitterly mourned her death and regretted that she didn't live to become first lady. He ordered fresh flowers daily, to be put before her portrait in the White House. He lived almost seven years after her death and died two years after leaving office.

Caroline Scott Harrison was born on October 1, 1832. She was a music teacher, an accomplished pianist, and a talented artist. As first lady, she renovated the White House and wanted to rebuild or add on to the present executive manor. This never occurred during her lifetime. She was instrumental in the first White House Christmas tree, and electric lights and wiring were installed in the executive manor while Caroline was first lady. Photography was also new and very much in vogue at the time the Harrisons occupied the White House, and many White House photographs were taken during his presidency. Caroline Harrison died as first lady on October 25, 1892, two weeks before Election Day. Benjamin Harrison thus became the second president whose wife died while he was in office. Running for election to his second term, both President Harrison and Grover Cleveland stopped campaigning, and Grover Cleveland won that election. Harrison left the White House in despair, still grieving his wife's death. However, he became the third widowed president to remarry when he wed Mary Dimmick on April 6, 1896. Mary was his wife's niece and 25 years younger than he was. They had one child, Elizabeth, who was younger than his own four grandchildren were. Mary Harrison lived until 1948.

Alice Lee Roosevelt was born on July 29, 1861. A charming, pretty, and intelligent 19-year-old, she married Theodore Roosevelt in 1880. On February 12, 1884 she gave birth to her namesake, Alice Lee Roosevelt, and died two days later from childbirth complications. Also on February 14, 1884, Theodore Roosevelt's mother died of typhoid in the same house. Teddy Roosevelt wrote in his diary, "the light has gone out of my life". He left his infant daughter with an aunt and moved west to the Dakotas. Returning later, he married Edith Carow, who had been born 10 days after his first wife. He thus became the fourth widowed-president to remarry, and he and Edith had five children. Daughter Alice Lee Roosevelt married in the White House in a most spectacular event on February 17, 1906, when her father was president and Edith Roosevelt was first lady.

Ellen Axson Wilson was born on May 15, 1860 and married Woodrow Wilson on June 24, 1885. During her term as first lady, she was active in helping eliminate the slums and poverty in Washington, D.C. She was instrumental in getting the "Alley" Bill before Congress and asked on her deathbed that the bill be passed. A frail woman, she died of Bright's disease, while first lady, on August 6, 1914. Her death was a shattering blow to President Wilson, as he was extremely devoted to her. He was so devastated that he stated he hoped to be assassinated and sat beside her body for two full days. He wrote of her death the next day, "God has stricken me almost beyond what I can bear". Thus President Wilson became the third president widowed while in office. As stricken as he was, he married Edith Bolling Galt, a widow for eight years, on December 18, 1915 while still in office. He was the only president to have two first ladies while in office. Edith died on December 28, 1961 on the one hundred and fifth anniversary of President Wilson's birth.

Lou Henry Hoover was born on March 29, 1874 and married Herbert Hoover on February 10, 1899. Both Lou and Herbert had spent the first 10 years of their lives in Iowa before moving to the West Coast to California and Oregon. They met at Stanford University, both as geology students. As well as being a fine horsewoman, Lou was interested in rocks, minerals, and mining. Immediately after their marriage, they left for China, where Herbert Hoover was serving as a mining engineer. Lou became proficient in Chinese and actually spoke five languages. During her years as first lady, she was involved in many charities and also served as the National Girl Scout President. The Hoovers spent eleven years of retirement together after leaving the White House. Lou Hoover died on January 7, 1944 of a heart attack. She was originally buried in California, but, when President Hoover died twenty years later, she was reinterred in Iowa. After her death, President Hoover realized just how many people she had really helped. In her drawer was a stack of uncashed checks received from people that she had helped during the Depression. Some believe that she died of a broken heart over how the nation blamed her husband for the severe depression. She died before President Hoover regained his reputation with the help of President Truman.

Thelma Ryan Nixon was born on March 16, 1912 and dubbed "Pat" by her father, because the next day was St. Patrick's Day. She spent her childhood in poverty, having been born in a mining shack in Nevada, and was orphaned by age 18. She met Richard Nixon in a theater production. Although called "plastic Pat" by journalists, she was a woman of great compassion. Helen Thomas, a White House reporter, said of Pat Nixon, she was the "warmest first lady I covered". In Vietnam she had a helicopter take her 18 miles into the jungle to see the wounded in the hospital and went bed to bed and talked to the injured soldiers. She served as first lady during the time of nationwide anti-war protests against the Vietnam War. Pat urged her husband to destroy the White House tapes, as she viewed them as personal, not public property. He ignored her warnings and she stood by as he announced his resignation on August 8, 1974, to take place "at noon tomorrow". Pat loathed politics and hated the role of first lady but did it for the man she loved. She suffered a mild stroke on July 7, 1976 and a milder one in 1983. She died on June 22, 1993 and President Nixon, survived her by only 10 months, as he died on April 22, 1994.

Barbara Pierce was born June 2, 1925 in Manhattan, New York. She married George Herbert Walker Bush on January 6, 1945 as a 19 year old. She became the second First Lady to be the wife of of one President and the mother of another. She and her husband, George Bush, lost a young child, Pauline Robinson, known as Robin, in 1953 of leukemia. Former First Lady, Barbara Bush, died on April 17, 2018 in Houston, Texas of complications from COPD. GHW Bush became the 16th US President to be called, Mr. President, widower. President Bush lived only seven and a half months dying on November 30, 2018.

Eleanor Rosalyn Smith was born on August 18, 1927. She also married the future president at a very young age on July 7, 1946. She was born, married and died in Plains, Georgia. Before her death on November 19, 2023, her husband, Jimmy Carter, had been on hospice due to his decision to no longer be treated for his cancer. Former President Jimmy Carter celebrated his 100th birthday on October 1, 2024 as a widower. He has lived to be the oldest president ever in the United States, and died on December 29, 2024, surviving Rosalyn by 13 months.

CHAPTER 2

DIED IN OFFICE

Eight presidents served full terms before the night William Henry Harrison died in office. He was to be the first of eight presidents who died in office. After his death in 1841, every third or fourth president died in office through John F. Kennedy in 1963. Since President Kennedy, seven presidents have served out their terms, with the exception of Nixon, who resigned. Zachary Taylor was the only president, of the eight who died in office, who was not elected in the "every-twenty-year curse", from 1840 to 1960.

From Taylor's death in 1850 to Harding's death in 1923, every fourth president died in office. Taylor was the twelfth president, Lincoln was the sixteenth, Garfield was the twentieth, McKinley was the twenty-fourth, and Harding was the twenty-eighth. Three presidents after Harding was Franklin Delano Roosevelt, who died in office, and then three presidents later was John F. Kennedy, who was assassinated while in office. Four of the eight, Lincoln, Garfield, McKinley and Kennedy, died from assassin's bullets. The other four, Harrison, Taylor, Harding and Roosevelt, died due to health reasons.

William Henry Harrison died only one month after taking office, after giving the longest inaugural speech in presidential history, on a cold, damp day, without wearing an overcoat. He caught a cold and it is believed this led to his death only a month later.

Zachary Taylor died only 5 days after the 4th of July, with speculation that he suffered food poisoning, sunburn, or was poisoned by his wife.

After a cross-country tour, President Harding suffered a heart attack on his return to Washington. As his condition grew worse, he attempted to recuperate in San Francisco, but died there of a massive stroke.

Franklin Delano Roosevelt, the only president to be elected to four terms, died of a cerebral hemorrhage in Warm Springs, Georgia on April 12th, 1945, the day before he was to broadcast a speech. Having presided as president through the Great Depression and World War II, he died only shortly before victory in Europe and victory in Japan brought World War II to an end.

The first president to be assassinated, Abraham Lincoln, was shot by John Wilkes Booth at Ford's Theater. Although he was shot on April 14th, 1865, he did not die until the next day.

Four presidents and not quite twenty years later, James Garfield was shot twice by Charles Guiteau at a railroad station in Washington on July 2nd, 1881. President Garfield survived for two and a half months, but finally died on September 19th.

Four presidents and five days short of twenty years later, a third president-lay dead from an assassin's bullet. Eight days earlier, on September 6th, 1901, President McKinley was shot by Leon Czolgosz during a speaking engagement at the Pan American Exposition in Buffalo, New York.

On November 22, 1963, a fourth assassin's bullets felled an American president. John Fitzgerald Kennedy died shortly after Lee Harvey Oswald's bullets reached him in a motorcade in Dallas, Texas. Two days later, a shocked nation watched live coverage on television of Jack Ruby shooting and killing Lee Harvey Oswald.

LEVEL I PRESIDENTIAL QUIZ

1. Name the first president.
2. Name the president who served the longest term.
3. Name the president who was assassinated in 1963.
4. Name the president who was assassinated in 1865.
5. Name the president who had polio.
6. Name the president during the Civil War.
7. Name the president whose First Lady was named LadyBird.
8. Name the presidents during World War II.
9. Who is buried in Grant's tomb?
10. Name the only two presidents who have been impeached (both were acquitted).
11. In what election year did it take 35 days to determine who won the election?
12. Name the only First Lady elected to the U.S. Senate
13. Name two presidents who were born in 1946.
14. On what date did the Whitewater-Monica Lewinski investigation of Bill Clinton finally end?

LEVEL II PRESIDENTIAL QUIZ

1. Name the only two presidents who signed the Declaration of Independence.

2. Who was the first president to die in office?

3. Name two sets of presidents who were father and son.

4. Name three presidents named George.

5. What was the last name of the man whose father and son were both presidents?

6. Who was the president responsible for the Louisiana Purchase?

7. Which president was the first to be widowed?

8. How many presidents have died in office?

9. Name two presidents in office during the Vietnam War.

10. Name two presidents married to women named Martha.

11. Name the only president who was never married.

12. Name the president who served during the 444 days that Iran held Americans hostage.

13. Who was the first president born in a hospital?

14. Which president was the first to have a beard?

15. Which president had the first telephone in the White House?

CHAPTER 3

ADMITTED TO THE BAR

An overwhelming majority of United States Presidents have been lawyers (27), before entering politics. Following are the years that they were admitted to the Bar:

John Adams, 1758 in Massachusetts
Thomas Jefferson, 1767
James Madison, in Virginia
James Monroe, 1786 in Virginia
John Quincy Adams, 1790 in Massachusetts
Andrew Jackson, 1787 in North Carolina
Martin Van Buren, 1803 in New York
John Tyler, 1809 in Virginia
James Polk, 1820 in Tennessee
Millard Fillmore, 1823 in New York
Franklin Pierce, 1827 in New Hampshire
James Buchanan, 1812 in Pennsylvania
Abraham Lincoln, 1836 in Illinois
Rutherford B. Hayes, 1845 in Ohio
James Garfield, 1860 in Ohio
Chester Arthur, 1854 in New York

Grover Cleveland, 1859 in New York
Benjamin Harrison, 1853 in Ohio
William McKinley, 1867 in Ohio
William Taft, 1880 in Ohio
Woodrow Wilson, 1882 in Georgia
Calvin Coolidge, 1897 in Massachusetts
Franklin D. Roosevelt, 1907 in New York
Richard Nixon, 1937 in California
Gerald Ford, 1941 in Michigan
Bill Clinton, 1973 in Arkansas
Barack Obama in Illinois

Theodore Roosevelt graduated from Harvard in 1880 and studied law at Columbia Law School in 1880-81, but was never admitted to the bar. His life was devoted to government service starting in 1882.

The second most popular occupation of our U.S. presidents was military service. General George Washington, of course, was an Army officer (he was, however, a surveyor by trade). William Henry Harrison, Zachary Taylor, Ulysses S. Grant, and Dwight D. Eisenhower also had careers as soldiers.

Andrew Johnson was a tailor. Warren Harding was a newspaper publisher. Herbert Hoover was a mining engineer. Harry Truman was a banker, farmer, soldier, and haberdasher. Lyndon Johnson was a teacher, Jimmy Carter a peanut farmer, and Ronald Reagan an actor. Both Bushes were in the oil business.

CHAPTER 4

GOVERNORS

Seventeen presidents were formerly governors of ten states: four of New York, three of Virginia, two each of Tennessee and Ohio, and one each of New Jersey, Massachusetts, Georgia, California, Arkansas, and Texas. New York governors were Van Buren, Cleveland, and both Roosevelts. Martin Van Buren was only governor a short time (January 1, 1829 to March 12, 1829), due to his resignation to accept appointment by Jackson as Secretary of State. Grover Cleveland was governor of New York from 1883 to 1885, Theodore Roosevelt from 1899 to 1901, and Franklin Delano Roosevelt from 1929 to 1933.

Thomas Jefferson, James Monroe, and John Tyler were all governors of Virginia: Jefferson from 1779 to 1781, Monroe from 1799 to 1803 and again in 1811 (resigning to accept appointment by Madison as Secretary of State), and Tyler from 1825 to 1827.

James Polk and Andrew Johnson were both governors of Tennessee: Polk from 1839 to 1841 and Andrew Johnson from 1853 to 1857.

Rutherford B. Hayes served as governor of Ohio from 1868 to 1872 and 1876 to 1877, while William McKinley was Ohio's governor from 1892 to 1896.

Woodrow Wilson was governor of New Jersey from 1911 to 1913; Calvin Coolidge was governor of Massachusetts from 1919 to 1920; Jimmy Carter was governor of Georgia from 1971 to 1975; Ronald Reagan was sworn in as governor of California in 1967 and sworn in for a second term in 1971. Bill Clinton was governor of Arkansas two separate times, from 1979 to 1981 and 1983 to 1992, losing the election in between. George W. Bush was Governor of Texas for six years before becoming President (1995-2000).

LEVEL III PRESIDENTIAL QUIZ

1. What does the "S" in Harry S Truman stand for?

2. Who was the last president born in a log cabin?

3. Name two presidents named Franklin.

4. Name two presidents who were bachelors when inaugurated.

5. Name the only president born in Pennsylvania.

6. Who was the largest president?

7. Who was the smallest president?

8. Who was the only president who was also a Chief Justice of the Supreme Court?

9. Who was president when Alaska and Hawaii were admitted to the Union?

10. Three of the first five presidents died on July 4th. Who were they?

11. Who was president for one month?

12. Who was the youngest president ever sworn in?

13. Who was the youngest president ever elected?

14. Who was president during WWI?

15. Who was president during the Korean War?

16. Who was president during the Gulf War?

17. Who was the oldest president?

18. Who was the first president to ride in an automobile?

19. Who was the first president to fly in an airplane?

20. Who was the first president to shake hands?

CHAPTER 5

TERMS

George Washington served two terms, all in the 18th Century. He was first inaugurated president on April 30, 1789 and retired from the presidency on March 3, 1797, thus shorting his eight full years by two months.

In the 19th Century, five presidents served eight consecutive years or two full terms. Jefferson was president from March 4, 1801 to March 3, 1809. Madison served in the Executive Office from March 4, 1809 to March 3, 1817. Monroe followed with his two terms from March 4, 1817 to March 3, 1825. Jackson was the fourth president to serve for a full eight years, from March 4, 1829 to March 3, 1837. Two consecutive terms were not again served until Ulysses S. Grant, who was in office from March 4, 1869 to March 3, 1877.

Grover Cleveland served two terms, but not consecutively, from March 4, 1885 to March 3, 1889 and March 4, 1893 to March 3, 1897.

Five presidents in the 20th Century also served two complete terms (including Franklin Delano Roosevelt's unprecedented election to a fourth term). Woodrow Wilson was inaugurated on March 4, 1913 and filled the Executive Office until March 3, 1921. Dwight Eisenhower was president from January 20, 1953 to January 20, 1961, and Ronald Reagan served eight years from January 20, 1981 to January 20, 1989. Bill Clinton completed two full terms from January 20, 1993 to January 20, 2001. One more president has held one full term than the number of presidents who have served two full terms. The 21st century has started with George W. Bush serving two full terms from January 20, 2001 to January 20, 2009 and Barack Obama serving two terms from January 20, 2009 to January 20, 2017.

One Term Presidents

John Adams - March 4, 1797 to March 3, 1801.
John Quincy Adams - March 4, 1825 to March 3, 1829.
Martin Van Buren - March 4, 1837 to March 3, 1841.

James Polk - March 4, 1845 to March 3, 1849.

Franklin Pierce - March 4, 1853 to March 3, 1857.

James Buchanan - March 4, 1857 to March 3, 1861.

Rutherford B. Hayes - March 4, 1877 to March 3, 1881.

Benjamin Harrison - March 4, 1889 to March 3, 1893.

William Howard Taft - March 4, 1909 to March 3, 1913.

Herbert Hoover - March 4, 1929 to March 3, 1933.

Jimmy Carter January 20, 1977 to January 20, 1981.

George Bush - January 20, 1989 to January 20, 1993.

Donald J. Trump - January 20, 2017 to January 20, 2021.

Joseph Biden - January 20, 2021 to January 20, 2025.

John Adams was defeated by Jefferson in the election of 1800, although he had hoped to serve two terms. John Quincy Adams was also defeated, running for his second term, in the 1828 election of Andrew Jackson. Martin Van Buren was defeated by William Henry Harrison in the 1840 election. James Polk wished to retire after one term and did not seek re-election. In the election of 1856, James Buchanan captured the Democratic nomination over incumbent President Pierce. Buchanan was not renominated by his party for the election of 1860.

Rutherford B. Hayes did not wish a second term as president and made that known at the beginning of his first term in 1877. Benjamin Harrison was defeated in the election of 1892, when Grover Cleveland won his second term and the only non-consecutive terms in presidential history, until Donald Trump. First Lady Caroline Harrison had died unexpectedly in October of that election year and the campaigning of all candidates stopped.

Abraham Lincoln was the first president assassinated in office, shot by John Wilkes Booth on April 14, 1865. He died the following day on April 15. His term began on March 4, 1861 and was a month and a half into his second term when he was killed. Andrew Johnson was sworn in as president on April 15, 1865 and completed that term to March 3, 1869. Almost twenty years later, the second president killed by an assassin's bullet was James Garfield. He was shot by Charles Guiteau on July 1, 1881, but lingered until his death on September 19. Chester Arthur became president on September 20, 1881, completing the term until March 3, 1885. Almost exactly twenty years later, a third assassin's bullet felled a U.S. President. Leon Czolgosz shot President McKinley on September 6, 1901 at the Pan American Exposition in Buffalo, New York. McKinley lived for eight days, dying on September 14, 1901. Theodore "Teddy" Roosevelt was sworn in on that day as the youngest president ever, at the age of 42. He completed that term and was elected in his own right to a second term and served until March 3, 1909.

After becoming president on March 4, 1921, Warren Harding died in office in San Francisco on August 2, 1923. Calvin Coolidge entered the Executive Office on August 3, 1923, completed that term, and was reelected in his own right, completing his presidency on March 3, 1929. Only a month after being sworn in for an unprecedented fourth term, Franklin Delano Roosevelt died on April 12, 1945 just as World War II was coming to an end. Harry Truman thus became president on April 12, 1945, was reelected in a surprise victory over Thomas Dewey, and served as president until January 20, 1953.

The fourth presidential assassination shocked the nation when John F. Kennedy was shot and killed by Lee Harvey Oswald, on November 22, 1963 in Dallas, Texas. Lyndon Baines Johnson was sworn in hours later aboard Air Force One, with Jacqueline Kennedy at his side. He won the election of 1964 and finished his term of office on January 20, 1969. On August 8, 1974, Richard Nixon announced his resignation, to take place "at noon tomorrow". Nixon was the first president to ever resign the office. Gerald Ford became president on August 9, 1974, completing the term on January 20, 1977. Ford had been named Vice President after Spiro Agnew resigned a year earlier and thus was the only U.S. President ever to hold that position without being elected by the people as either.

CHAPTER 6

FIRST LADIES

From Martha to Jill, we Americans have been fascinated by our first ladies for over two centuries. Although, the term "First Lady" was not widely used until a play about Dolley Madison in 1911 called "First Lady of the Land".

Jill Biden was the 41st First Lady (or 42nd if Frances Cleveland is counted twice), although the 57th White House hostess. Daughters, sisters, nieces have filled the role when presidents were widows or in the case of President Buchanan, never married. Only one president, Woodrow Wilson, had two first ladies while president, Ellen and Edith, after his marriage to Edith following Ellen's death. Besides the only bachelor president, James Buchanan, Thomas Jefferson, Andrew Jackson, Martin Van Buren, and Chester Arthur were widowed before taking office.

First ladies have historically struggled to balance the commoner/queen role as the early culture was somewhat patterned after English custom. In the first century of the presidency, Dolley Madison was held up as the First Lady to emulate. Jacqueline Kennedy was probably the most queen-like of the First Ladies of the second century.

Eleanor Roosevelt was the most active first lady, followed consecutively by the least active, Bess Truman. Michelle Obama is the second first lady with a law degree, following Hillary Clinton.

Four out of the last nine first ladies have had two daughters; Lady Bird Johnson: Lynda Bird and Lucy Baines, Pat Nixon: Tricia and Julie, Laura Bush: Jenna and Barbara, and Michelle Obama: Malia and Sasha. Laura Bush is the only first lady to have twins. Chelsea Clinton was of course an only girl and Amy Carter was the only child of Rosalyn and Jimmy Carter to live in the White House as her older siblings were all grown. The last male child to live in the White House prior to Barron Trump was John John, John Fitzgerald Kennedy, Jr., whom America tragically lost in a plane crash before the turn of the century. Carter's other children, Ford's, Reagan's and G.H.W. Bush's were not children when their fathers' were president.

Two first ladies never lived in the White House. Abigail Adams was the first to live in the White House as it wasn't built during Washington's two terms. Thus Martha Washington, called Lady Washington by the press was one of two to not live in the White House. The second was Anna Harrison. She was delayed by an illness to travel to Washington to join her husband, President Harrison, and never made it as he died 30 days after his inauguration

Two first ladies have had a seat in Congress. Hillary Clinton, was elected and served as senator of New York prior to becoming Secretary of State in Obama's administration. Dolley Madison was given an honorary seat on the floor of Congress.

Melania Trump becomes the second First Lady to not be born in the United States. She was born Melania Knauss (Americanized spelling of her birth name) in Slovenia, Yugoslavia on April 26,1970. She speaks six languages; Serbo-Croatian, English, French, Italian, German, and Slovene.

The First Ladies Library opened in 1999 in First Lady Ida McKinley's former home. The National First Ladies Library is in Canton, Ohio.

First Lady Firsts

1. First to live in the White House Abigail Adams
2. First to respond to a telegraph message Dolley Madison
3. First to speak a foreign language fluently (French) Elizabeth Monroe
4. First to be born in a foreign country (England) Louisa Adams
5. First to work and earn a salary before marriage Abigail Fillmore
6. First to host the Easter Egg Roll Lucy Hayes
7. First to marry a sitting president Frances Cleveland
8. First to use electricity Caroline Harrison
9. First to have a Christmas tree in White House Caroline Harrison
10. First to own and drive a car Nellie Taft
11. First to fly in an airplane Florence Harding
12. First to own a radio Florence Harding
13. First to vote Florence Harding
14. First to hold regular press conferences Eleanor Roosevelt
15. First to appear in television commercial during campaign Mamie Eisenhower
16. First to hire a press secretary Jacqueline Kennedy
17. First to wear pants in public Pat Nixon
18. First to have a VCR in the White House Rosalyn Carter
19. First to become Secretary of State Hillary Clinton
20. First African American First Lady Michelle Obama
21. First to speak six languages Melania Trump
22. Dr. Jill Biden was the first First Lady with a doctorate degree and the first to be employed while serving as First Lady.

CHAPTER 7

MARRIAGES AND CHILDREN

Only one president, James Buchanan, never married. Six of the remaining forty-five men who have been president were married twice. Donald Trump was married three times. One, Ronald Reagan, married after being divorced, and the other five remarried after being widowed. Those five were Tyler, Fillmore, Benjamin Harrison, Theodore Roosevelt, and Wilson.

George Washington married Martha Dandridge Custis on January 6, 1759 in New Kent County, Virginia. He was twenty-six years old at the time of the marriage; Martha had been widowed from her first husband and had given birth to four children, two of whom died in infancy. George and Martha had no children of their own.

John Adams married Abigail Smith at age 28 on October 25, 1764, at Weymouth, Massachusetts. John and Abigail had 5 children, one of whom died in infancy. Abigail Amelia was born on July 14, 1765, John Quincy Adams was born on July 11, 1767, Susanna was born on December 28, 1768 and died on February 4, 1770, Charles was born on May 29, 1770, and Thomas Boylston was born on September 15, 1772.

Thomas Jefferson married Martha Wayles Skelton on January 1, 1772 in Williamsburg, Virginia. Jefferson was 28 at the time of his marriage to Martha, who was previously married and widowed. She had one child born to her first marriage (a son), who died before she and Thomas were married. Thomas and Martha had six children, four of whom died in infancy. Martha Washington was born on September 27, 1772; Jane Randolph was born on April 3, 1774 and died in 1775; an unnamed son was born on May 28,1777 and died two weeks later on June 14; Mary was born on August 1, 1778; Lucy Elizabeth was born on November 3, 1780 and died in 1781; a second Lucy Elizabeth was born on May 8, 1782 and died in 1785.

James Madison was 43 years old when he married Dolley Dandridge Payne Todd. They were married on September 15, 1794 in Jefferson County, Virginia. Dolley had been widowed by Mr. Todd previous to her marriage to James Madison and had had two sons, one of whom died in infancy. James and Dolley had no children between them.

James Monroe was married at age 27 to Elizabeth Kortright on February 16, 1786 in New York, New York. James and Elizabeth had five children, one of whom died in infancy. Eliza Kortright was born in December 1786; an unnamed son was born in May 1799 and died in infancy; Maria Hesther was born in 1803.

John Quincy Adams married Louisa Catherine Johnson at age 30 on July 26, 1797 in London, England. John Quincy and Louisa had four children, one of whom died in infancy. George Washington was born on April 13, 1801; John was born on July 4, 1803; Charles Francis was born on August 18, 1807; Louisa Catherine was born in 1811 and died in 1812.

Andrew Jackson married Rachel Donelson Robards at age 24 in August of 1791. Rachel had been previously married to Lewis Robards and, at the time of her marriage to Andrew, they believed that she was divorced. When it was later learned that the divorce had not been final, a second ceremony took place on January 17, 1794 in Nashville, Tennessee. Rachel had no children with either Mr. Robards or Andrew Jackson.

Martin Van Buren married Hannah Hoes at age 24 on February 21, 1807 in Catskill, New York. Martin and Hannah had four children, all of whom lived to adulthood. Abraham was born on November 27, 1807; John was born on February 18, 1810; Martin was born on December 20, 1812; Smith Thompson was born on January 16, 1817.

William Henry Harrison married Anna Tuthill Symmes at age 22 on November 25, 1795 in North Bend, Ohio. William and Anna had 10 children, nine of whom lived to adulthood. Elizabeth Bassett was born on September 29, 1796; John Cleves Symmes was born on October 28, 1798; Lucy Singleton was born in September, 1800; William Henry was born on September 3, 1802; John Scott was born on October 4, 1804; Benjamin was born in 1806; Mary Symmes was born on January 22, 1809; Carter Bassett was born on October 26, 1811; Anna Tuthill was born on October 28, 1813; their last child, James Findlay, was born in 1814 and died in 1817.

John Tyler was 23 years old when he married his first wife, Letitia Christian, on March 29, 1813 in New Kent County, Virginia. John and Letitia had eight children, one of whom died in infancy. Mary was born on April 15, 1815, Robert on September 9, 1816, John on April 27, 1819, Letitia on May 11, 1821, and Elizabeth on July 11, 1823. Anne Contesse was born in April, 1825 and died in July of the same year. Alice was born on March 23, 1827, and Tazewell was born on December 6, 1830. Tyler's wife, Letitia, died on September 10, 1842 and he married Julia Gardiner on June 26, 1844 at age 54, in New York, New York. John and Julia had seven children, all of whom lived to adulthood. David Gardiner was born on July 12, 1846, John Alexander on April 7, 1848, Julia on December 25, 1849, and Lachlan on December 2, 1851. Lyon Gardiner was born in August of 1853. Robert Fitzwalter was born on March 12, 1856, and Pearl was born on June 20, 1860.

James Polk married Sarah Childress at age 28 on January 1, 1824 in Murfreesboro, Tennessee. James and Sarah had no children.

Zachary Taylor married Margaret Mackall Smith at age 25 on June 21, 1810 near Louisville, Kentucky. Zachary and "Peggy", as she was called, had six children, two of whom died in infancy. Anne Margaret Mackall was born on April 9, 1811; Sarah Knox was born on March 6, 1814; Octavia Pannel was born on August 16, 1816 and died in 1820; Margaret Smith was born on July 27, 1819 and also died in 1820; Mary Elizabeth was born on April 20, 1824; Richard was born on January 27, 1826.

Millard Fillmore married Abigail Powers at age 26 on February 5, 1826 in Moravia, New York. Millard and Abigail had two children: Millard Powers, born on April 25, 1828, and Mary Abigail, born on March 27, 1832. Abigail died on March 30, 1853 and Millard Fillmore married Caroline Carmichael McIntosh at age 58 on February 10, 1858 in Albany, New York. Caroline was the widow of Mr. McIntosh. She and Millard had no children.

Franklin Pierce married Jane Means Appleton at age 29 on November 10, 1834 in Amherst, Massachusetts. Franklin and Jane had three sons, none of whom lived to adulthood. Franklin was born on February 2, 1836 and died three days later; Frank Robert was born on August 27, 1839 and died in 1843; Benjamin was born on April 13, 1841 and died in 1853.

Abraham Lincoln married Mary Todd at age 33 on November 4, 1842 in Springfield, Illinois. Mary and Abraham had four children, only one of who survived to adulthood. Robert Todd was born on August 1, 1843; Edward Baker was born on March 10, 1846 and died in 1850; William Wallace was born on December 21, 1850 and died in 1862; Thomas, commonly known as "Tad", was born on April 4, 1853 and died in 1871.

Andrew Johnson married Eliza McCardle at age 18 on May 17, 1827 in Greeneville, Tennessee. Andrew and Eliza had five children, all of whom survived to adulthood. Martha was born on October 25, 1828; Charles on February 19, 1830; Mary on May 8, 1832; Robert on February 22, 1834; and Andrew on August 5, 1852.

Ulysses S. Grant married Julia Boggs Dent at age 26 on August 22, 1848 in St. Louis, Missouri. Julia and Ulysses had four children: Frederick Dent on May 30, 1850; Ulysses Simpson on July 22, 1852; Ellen Wrenshall on July 4, 1855; and Jesse Root on February 6, 1858.

Rutherford B. Hayes married Lucy Ware Webb at age 30 on December 30, 1852 in Cincinnati, Ohio. Rutherford and Lucy had eight children, three of whom died in infancy. Birchard Austin was born on November 4, 1853; James Webb Cook was born on March 20, 1856; Rutherford Platt was born on June 24, 1858; Joseph Thompson was born on December 21, 1861 and died in 1863; George Crook was born on September 29, 1864 and died in 1866; Fanny was born on September 2, 1867; Scott Russell was born on February 8, 1871; Manning Force was born on August 1, 1873 and died in 1874.

James Garfield married Lucretia Rudolph at age 26 on November 11, 1858 in Hiram, Ohio. James and Lucretia had seven children, two of whom died in infancy. Eliza Arabella was born on July 3, 1860 and died in 1863; Harry Augustus was born on October 11, 1863; James Rudolph on October 17, 1865; Mary on January 16, 1867; Irvin McDowell on August 3, 1870; Abram on November 21, 1872. Edward was born on December 25, 1874 and died in 1876.

Chester Arthur married Ellen Lewis Herndon at age 30 on October 25, 1859 in New York, New York. Ellen and Chester had three children, their first dying in infancy. William Lewis Herndon was born on December 10, 1860 and died in 1863; Chester Alan was born on July 25, 1864; and Ellen Herndon was born on November 21, 1871.

Grover Cleveland married Frances Folsom at age 49 on June 2, 1886 in Washington, D.C. Grover Cleveland was a bachelor when he was inaugurated for his first term as president. Frances and Grover had five children, four of whom lived to adulthood. Ruth was born on October 3, 1891 and died in 1904; Esther was born on September 9, 1893; Marion on July 7, 1895; Richard Folsom on October 28, 1897; and Francis Grover on July 18, 1903.

Benjamin Harrison was married to Caroline Lavinia Scott at age 20 on October 20, 1853. Caroline and Benjamin had two children: Russell Benjamin, born on August 12, 1854, and Mary Scott, born on April 3, 1858. Caroline died on October 25, 1892, and Benjamin married Mary Scott Lord Dimmick at age 62 on April 6, 1896 in New York, New York. Benjamin and Mary had one daughter, Elizabeth, born on February 21, 1897.

William McKinley married Ida Saxton at age 27 on January 25th, 1871 in Canton, Ohio. Ida and William had two children, both of whom died in infancy. Katherine was born on their first wedding anniversary, January 25, 1872 and died in 1875. Ida was born on March 31, 1873 and died five months later in August.

Theodore Roosevelt married Alice Hathaway Lee on his 22nd birthday, October 27, 1880, in Brookline, Massachusetts. Alice and Theodore had one child, Alice Lee, born on February 12, 1884. Wife Alice died on February 14, 1884 and Theodore married Edith Kermit Carow on December 2, 1886 in London, England, at age 28. Edith and Theodore had five children, all of whom survived to adulthood. Theodore was born on September 13, 1887; Kermit on October 10, 1889; Ethel Carow on August 13, 1891; Archibald Bulloch on April 9, 1894; and Quentin on November 19, 1897.

William Taft married Helen Herron at age 28 on June 19, 1886 in Cincinnati, Ohio. Helen and William had three children, all of whom lived to adulthood. Robert Alphonso was born on September 8, 1889: Helen Herron on August 1, 1891; and Charles Phelps on September 20, 1897.

Woodrow Wilson married Ellen Louise Axson at age 28 on June 24, 1885 in Savannah, Georgia. Ellen and Woodrow had three children: Margaret Woodrow on April 30, 1886; Jessie Woodrow on August 28, 1887; and Eleanor Randolph on October 16, 1889. Ellen died on August 6, 1914 and, at age 58, Woodrow Wilson married Edith Bolling Galt on December 18, 1915 in Washington, D.C. Edith was the widow of Norman Galt and had lost one child in infancy. She and Woodrow had no children.

Warren Harding married Florence Kling De Wolfe at age 25 on July 8, 1891 in Marion, Ohio. Florence was divorced in 1885 from Henry De Wolfe and had one son, Marshall. She and Warren had no children.

Calvin Coolidge married Grace Anna Goodhue at age 33 on October 4, 1905, in Burlington, Vermont. Grace and Calvin had two children: John, born on September 7, 1906 and Calvin, who was born on April 13, 1908 and died in 1924.

Herbert Hoover married Lou Henry at age 24 on February 10, 1899 in Monterey, California. Herbert and Lou had two children: Herbert Clark, born on August 4, 1903 and Allan Henry, born on July 17, 1907.

Franklin Delano Roosevelt married Anna Eleanor Roosevelt at age 23 on March 17, 1905, in New York, New York. Eleanor was a fifth cousin, once removed, to Franklin. Eleanor and Franklin had six children, one of whom died in infancy. Anna Eleanor was born on May 3, 1906; James was born on December 23, 1907; Franklin was born on March 18, 1909 and died later the same year; Elliott was born on September 23, 1910; Franklin Delano, Jr. on August 17, 1914; and John Aspinwall on March 13, 1916.

Harry Truman married Elizabeth Virginia ("Bess") Wallace at age 35 on June 28, 1919 in Independence, Missouri. Bess and Harry had one daughter, Mary Margaret, born on February 17, 1924.

Dwight Eisenhower married Marie Geneva ("Mamie") Doud at age 25 on July 1, 1916 in Denver, Colorado. Mamie and Dwight had two sons: Dwight Doud on September 24, 1917 and John Sheldon Doud on August 3, 1923.

John Kennedy married Jacqueline Lee ("Jackie") Bouvier at age 36 on September 12, 1953 in Newport, Rhode Island. Jackie and John had three children, one of whom died in infancy. Caroline Bouvier was born on November 27, 1957 and John Fitzgerald, Jr. was born on November 25, 1960. Patrick Bouvier was born on August 7, 1963 and died two days later.

Lyndon Johnson married Claudia Alta ("Lady Bird") Taylor at age 26 on November 17, 1934 in San Antonio, Texas. LadyBird and Lyndon had two daughters: Lynda Bird, born on March 19, 1944 and Lucy Baines, born on July 2, 1947.

Richard Nixon married Thelma Catherine ("Pat") Ryan at age 27 on June 21, 1940 in Riverside, California. Pat and Richard had two daughters: Patricia, known as Tricia, born on February 21, 1946 and Julie, born on July 5, 1948.

Gerald Ford married Elizabeth Bloomer Warren at age 35 on October 15, 1948 in Grand Rapids, Michigan. "Betty" had been divorced from William Warren in 1947. Betty and Gerald had four children: Michael Gerald, born on March 14, 1950; John Gardner, born on March 16, 1952; Steven Meigs, born on May 19, 1956; and Susan Elizabeth, born on July 6, 1957.

Jimmy Carter married Eleanor Rosalyn Smith at age 21 on July 7, 1946 in Plains, Georgia. "Rosalyn" and Jimmy had four children: John William, born on July 3, 1947; James Earl, born on April 12, 1950; Donnel Jeffery, born on August 18, 1952; and Amy Lynn, born on October 19, 1967.

Ronald Reagan married Sarah Jane Fulks, known by her celebrity and married name as Jane Wyman, at age 28 on January 24, 1940 in Glendale, California. Ronald and Jane had two children: Maureen Elizabeth, born on January 4, 1941 and Michael Edward (adopted), born in 1945. Daughter Christine was born June 26, 1947 and died the same day. Ronald and Jane were divorced on July 19, 1949 and Ronald married Anne Frances Robbins, known by her celebrity name as Nancy Davis, at age 41 on March 4, 1952 in Los Angeles, California. Nancy and Ronald had two children: Patricia Ann, born on October 21, 1952, and Ronald Prescott, born on May 20, 1958.

George Bush married Barbara Pierce at age 20 on January 6, 1945 in Rye, New York. Barbara and George had six children, five of whom lived to adulthood. George Walker was born on July 6, 1946; Robin was born on December 20, 1949 and died in 1953; John Ellis was born on February 11, 1953; Neil Mallon on January 22, 1955; Marvin Pierce on October 22, 1956; and Dorothy Pierce on August 18, 1959.

Bill Clinton married Hillary Rodham at age 29 on October 11, 1975. One child was born to this marriage: Chelsea, on February 27, 1980.

George W. Bush married Laura Welch at age 31 on November 5, 1977 in Midland, Texas. George and Laura had twin daughters, Barbara and Jenna (named after their two grandmothers) on November 25, 1981.

Barack Obama married Michelle LaVaughn Robinson at age 31 on October 18, 1992 in Chicago. Barack and Michelle had two daughters, Malia Ann, born on July 4, 1998 and Natasha (Sasha) born on June 10, 2001.

Donald Trump married Melania Knauss on January 22, 2005 in Florida. They have one son, Barron William Trump, born March 20, 2006. Trump has three children from his first marriage to Ivana Trump; Donald Jr. born December 31, 1977, Ivanka born October 30, 1981, and Eric born January 6, 1984. Daughter Tiffany was born to Marla Maples, his second wife, on October 13, 1993.

Joe Biden married Neilia Hunter on August 27, 1966. Three children were born to this marriage; Joseph Robynette Biden, III (Beau) on February 3, 1969; Robert Hunter Biden on February 4, 1970; and daughter Naomi Christina (Amy), who was killed in a car crash with her mother on April 12, 1972. President Biden married Jill on June 17, 1977 and their daughter Ashley was born on June 8, 1981..

CHAPTER 8

PRESIDENTIAL BIRTHS

Following is a chronological list of president's births, rather than their order as president:

George Washington - February 22nd, 1732
(or by the old calendar, February 11, 1732.)
John Adams - October 30, 1735.
Thomas Jefferson - April 13, 1743.
James Madison - March 16, 1751.
James Monroe - April 28, 1758.
Andrew Jackson - March 15, 1767.
John Quincy Adams - July 11, 1767.
William Henry Harrison - February 9, 1773.
Martin Van Buren - December 5, 1782.
Zachary Taylor - November 24, 1784.
John Tyler - March 29, 1790.
James Buchanan - April 23, 1791.
James Knox Polk - November 2, 1795.
Millard Fillmore - January 7, 1800.
Franklin Pierce - November 23, 1804.
Andrew Johnson - December 29, 1808.
Abraham Lincoln - February 12, 1809.
Ulysses S. Grant - April 27, 1822.
Rutherford B. Hayes - October 4, 1822.
Chester Alan Arthur - October 5, 1830.
James Abram Garfield - November 19, 1831.
Benjamin Harrison - August 20, 1833.
Steven Grover Cleveland - March 18, 1837.
William McKinley - January 29, 1843.
Thomas Woodrow Wilson December 28, 1856.

William Howard Taft - September 15, 1857.

Theodore Roosevelt - October 27, 1858.

Warren G. Harding - November 2, 1865.

John Calvin Coolidge - July 4, 1872.

Herbert Clark Hoover - August 10, 1874.

Franklin Delano Roosevelt - January 30, 1882.

Harry S Truman - May 8, 1884.

Dwight David Eisenhower - October 14, 1890.

Lyndon Baines Johnson - August 27, 1908.

Ronald Reagan - February 6, 1911.

Richard M. Nixon - January 9, 1913.

Gerald R. Ford - July 14, 1913.

John Fitzgerald Kennedy - May 29, 1917.

George Herbert Walker Bush - June 12, 1924.

James Earl Carter - October 1, 1924

Joe Biden - November 20, 1942

Donald John Trump - June 14, 1946

George Walker Bush - July 6, 1946

William Jefferson Clinton - August 19, 1946

Barack Hussein Obama - August 4, 1961

LEVEL IV PRESIDENTIAL QUIZ

1. What is the only decade since George Washington was born that no United States Presidents were born?

2. Name the two presidents who were born in 1767.

3. Name two presidents who were born in 1822.

4. Name two presidents who were born in 1913.

5. Name two presiderts born in 1924.

6. How many presidents were governors of states?

7. Name the only president that did not live in either the 1800s or the 1900s.

8. Who was president when 5 states were admitted to the Union, and name the 5 states?

9. What does the "B" stand for in Rutherford B. Hayes?

10. Which two presidents were married on their birthdays?

11. Name three presidents who died on the 22nd of the month, whose terms were consecutive to one another.

12. Name the first president to have a state or states admitted to the Union beyond the original 13 colonies.

13. Who was the president with the most children?

14. Name two presidents who were born with different names than their presidential names.

15. Arizona and New Mexico were the last two states admitted to the Union before Alaska and Hawaii. Who was president at the time of their admission?

16. Who was the first divorced president?

17. Which first lady lived to be the oldest, to age 97?

18. How many presidents were inaugurated on January 20th for their first term?

19. Who was the youngest First Lady?

20. Who are the four presidents carved into Mount Rushmore?

CHAPTER 9

PRESIDENTIAL DEATHS

Following is a chronological list of the dates of deaths of presidents in the order in which they died:

George Washington - December 14, 1799.

Thomas Jefferson July 4, 1826. [Last words: "Is it the fourth?"]

John Adams - July 4, 1826 (a few hours later). [As John Adams died he murmured "Thomas Jefferson still survives". He was wrong. Jefferson had died earlier unbeknownst to Adams.]

James Monroe - July 4, 1831.

James Madison - June 28, 1836.

William Henry Harrison - April 4, 1841.

Andrew Jackson - June 8, 1845.

John Quincy Adams - February 23, 1848.

James Knox Polk - June 15, 1849.

Zachary Taylor July 9, 1850.

John Tyler January 18, 1862.

Martin Van Buren - July 24, 1862.

Abraham Lincoln - April 15, 1865.

James Buchanan - June 1, 1868.

Franklin Pierce - October 8, 1869.

Millard Fillmore - March 8, 1874.

Andrew Johnson - July 31, 1875.

James A. Garfield - September 19, 1881.

Ulysses S. Grant - July 23, 1885.

Chester Arthur November 18, 1886.

Rutherford B. Hayes - January 17, 1893.

Benjamin Harrison - March 13, 1901.

William McKinley - September 14, 1901.

Grover Cleveland - June 24, 1908.

Theodore Roosevelt - January 6, 1919.

Warren Harding - August 2, 1923.

Woodrow Wilson - February 3, 1924.

William Howard Taft - March 8, 1930

Calvin Coolidge - January 5, 1933.

Franklin Delano Roosevelt - April 12, 1945.

John Kennedy - November 22, 1963.

Herbert Hoover October 20, 1964.

Dwight David Eisenhower - March 28, 1969.

Harry S Truman - December 26, 1972.

Lyndon Baines Johnson - January 22, 1973.

Richard Nixon - April 22, 1994

Ronald Reagan - June 5, 2004

Gerald Ford - December 26, 2006

Five former presidents were living the day George W. Bush was sworn in as president. They were Ford, Carter, Reagan, George H.W., and Clinton. Only three of those were alive when Obama was sworn in, Carter, GHW Bush, and Clinton. As Trump was sworn in, five former presidents were alive: Carter, GHW Bush, Clinton, GW Bush and Obama.

George Herbert Walker Bush - November 30, 2018

Jimmy Carter - December 29, 2024

CHAPTER 10

NATIVE STATES

An astonishing twenty-four presidents of the United States were born in only four states: Virginia, Ohio, Massachusetts, and New York. Over 50% of the forty-four men who have served in the executive office were born in less than 10% of the states.

Eight presidents were born in Virginia. George Washington was born in Pope's Creek, Westmoreland County, Virginia. Thomas Jefferson was born in Shadwell, Goochland County, now Albemarle County, Virginia. James Madison was born in Port Conway, Virginia. James Monroe was born in Westmoreland County, Virginia. William Henry Harrison was born in Berkeley, Charles City County, Virginia. John Tyler was born in Charles City County, Virginia. Zachary Taylor was born in Montebello, Orange County, Virginia. Woodrow Wilson was born in Staunton, Virginia.

Seven presidents were born in Ohio. Ulysses S. Grant was born in Point Pleasant, Ohio; Rutherford B. Hayes in Delaware, Ohio; and James Garfield in Orange, Ohio. Benjamin Harrison was born in North Bend, Ohio, and William McKinley was born in Niles, Ohio. William Howard Taft was born in Cincinnati, Ohio, and Warren Harding was born in Corsica, Ohio.

Both John Adams and John Quincy Adams were born in Braintree, Massachusetts, now Quincy, Massachusetts. John Kennedy was born in Brookline, Massachusetts and George Bush was born in Milton, Massachusetts.

Martin Van Buren was born in Kinderhook, New York. Millard Fillmore was born in Summerhill, Cayuga County, New York. Theodore Roosevelt was born in New York City, New York, Franklin Delano Roosevelt was born in Hyde Park, New York and Donald Trump was born in New York City (Queens). Two presidents each were born in North Carolina, Vermont, and Texas. James Polk and Andrew Johnson were both born in North Carolina; Polk in Mecklenburg County and Johnson in Raleigh. Presidents Arthur and Coolidge were both born in Vermont; Arthur in Fairfield and Coolidge in Plymouth. The two presidents born in Texas were Eisenhower and Lyndon Johnson; Eisenhower in Denison and Johnson near Stonewall, Texas. Two presidents were born in Pennsylvania; James Buchanan in Cove Gap and Joe Biden in Scranton. Two presidents were born in California; Richard Nixon in Yorba Linda.

Eleven other states have been the birthplace of one president each. Andrew Jackson was born in Waxhaw, South Carolina. Franklin Pierce was born in Hillsboro, New Hampshire. James Buchanan was born in Cove Gap, Pennsylvania. Abraham Lincoln was born in Hodgenville Hardin County (now Larue County), Kentucky. Grover Cleveland was born in Caldwell, New Jersey. Herbert Hoover was born in West Branch, Iowa. Harry Truman was born in Lamar, Missouri. Richard Nixon was born in Yorba Linda, California. Gerald Ford was born in Omaha, Nebraska. Jimmy Carter was born in Plains, Georgia. Ronald Reagan was born in Tampico, Illinois. William Clinton was born in Hope, Arkansas. George W. Bush was born in New Haven, Connecticut. Obama was born in Hawaii.

LEVEL V PRESIDENTIAL QUIZ

1. Who was the president whose first name was Stephen?
2. Name two presidents who served in the Congress after they were presidents.
3. Name the only state admitted during Jefferson's presidency.
4. Name the president whose father was the governor of New Hampshire.
5. Which president was in office when California was admitted to the Union?
6. Name four presidents married to Elizabeths or Elizas.
7. Name the only president married as a teenager.
8. Name a president who won a Nobel Peace Prize.
9. Name two first ladies whose first names were Eleanor.
10. Name five presidents whose first names were John.
11. Name two presidents whose first names were Thomas.
12. Name four presidents whose first names were William.
13. Which president proclaimed the first Thanksgiving?
14. Name the two presidents who had never been married when they were first inaugurated.
15. Which president had sons named Abraham, Martin, and John?
16. Which presidents became fathers after they left the White House?
17. Who was the first president born a citizen of the United States of America?
18. What was the population in the first U.S. Census in 1790, when George Washington was president?
19. Who was the first president to wear long pants?
20. A daughter of one of our presidents married Jefferson Davis, president of the Confederate States. Who was her father?

CHAPTER 11

STATES ADMITTED TO THE UNION

Thirty-seven states were admitted to the union after the original thirteen colonies, during seventeen presidencies. During President Washington's tenure, the first three states were admitted: Vermont in 1791; Kentucky in 1792; and Tennessee in 1796. Ohio was the only state admitted during Jefferson's term, in 1803. Louisiana and Indiana were admitted to the Union during James Madison's presidency; Louisiana in 1812 and Indiana in 1816. The United States was growing quickly as five states were admitted during the Monroe presidency; Mississippi in 1817, Illinois in 1818, Alabama in 1819, Maine in 1820, and Missouri in 1821.

Fifteen years passed before another state joined the Union. Arkansas was admitted in 1836 and Michigan in 1837 under Andrew Jackson. Only Florida was admitted while John Tyler was president in 1845. Texas, Iowa, and Wisconsin, admitted during the Polk administration, brought the total to thirty states. Texas was admitted in 1845, Iowa in 1846, and Wisconsin in 1848. Two years and two presidents later, California was admitted under President Millard Fillmore in 1850.

It was almost a decade before another state was admitted to the Union. Under James Buchanan's term, Minnesota became a state in 1858, Oregon in 1859, and Kansas in 1861. Two years later, during the Civil War, after Virginia had seceded to the Confederate States, certain counties remained loyal to the North (or the Union, as it was then called) and West Virginia became a state in 1863. Nevada joined the Union in 1864, both of these under President Lincoln. Only Nebraska was admitted to the Union while Andrew Johnson was president, in 1867.

It was almost another decade until Colorado joined the United States in 1876, during the presidency of Ulysses S. Grant. The most states ever admitted to the Union under one president were during Benjamin Harrison's four year term: North Dakota, South Dakota, Montana and Washington were all admitted in 1889; and Idaho and Wyoming in 1890. During Cleveland's second term, Utah was the only state to join the Union, in 1896.

The territory of Oklahoma had been originally set aside for Native Americans, who during that era were referred to as American Indians. Later, Oklahoma was involved in a land rush when it became open to claim staking. Oklahoma was admitted to the Union as a state in 1907 under Theodore Roosevelt. Completing the forty-eight contiguous states, New Mexico and Arizona were both admitted to the Union in 1912, under President Taft. It wasn't until 47 years later, under President Eisenhower, that Alaska and Hawaii were admitted in 1959, with Alaska becoming the 49th state and Hawaii the 50th and final state to date

MAPS

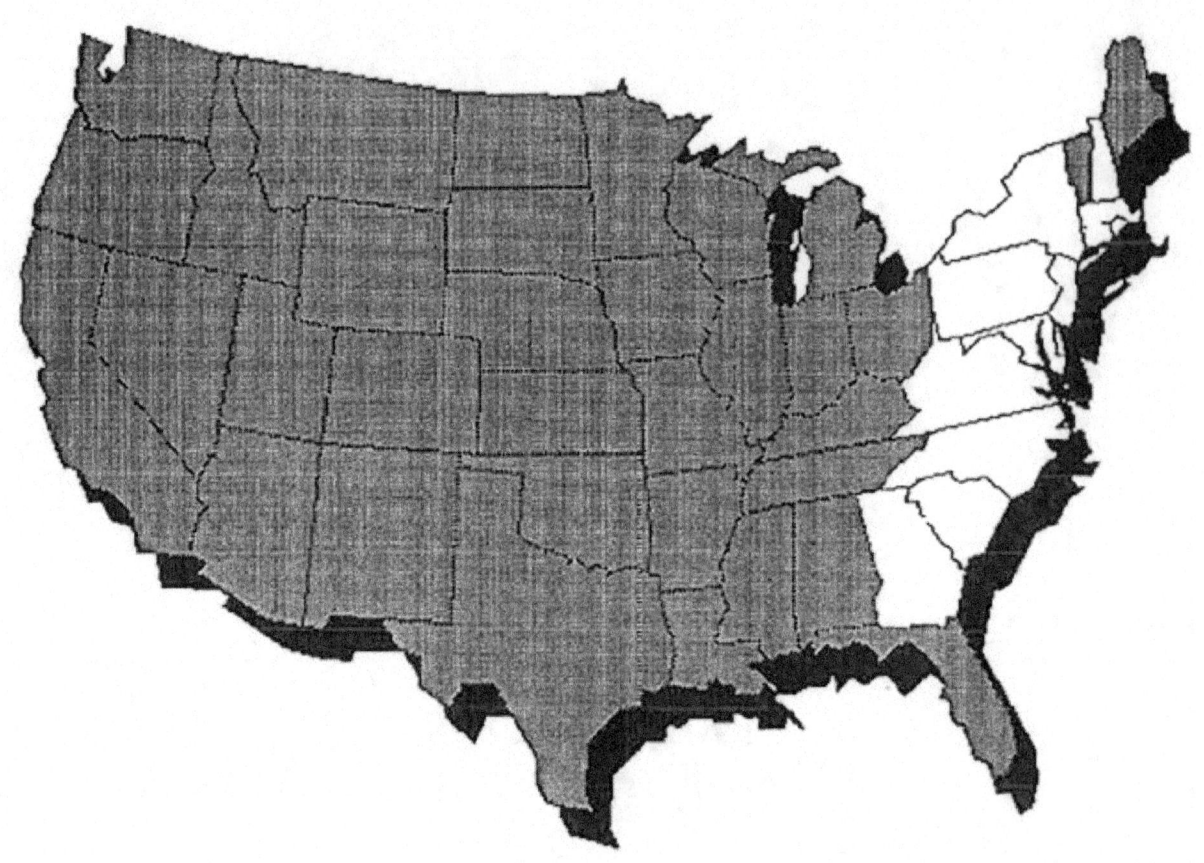

The Original Thirteen

New York

Massachusetts

Pennsylvania

North Carolina

New Hampshire

Delaware

Connecticut

South Carolina

Virginia

New Jersey

Rhode Island

Maryland

Georgia

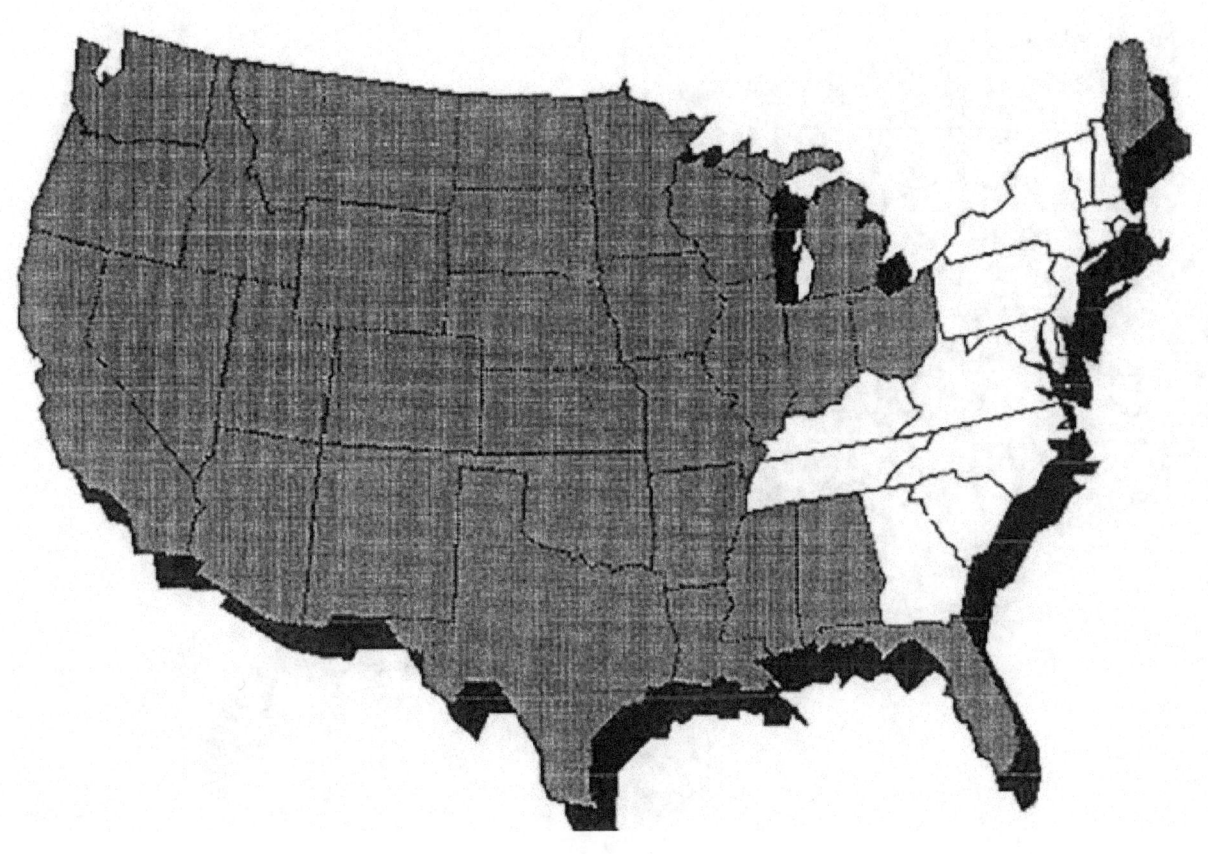

Washington's Presidency

Vermont 1791
Kentucky 1792
Tennessee 1796

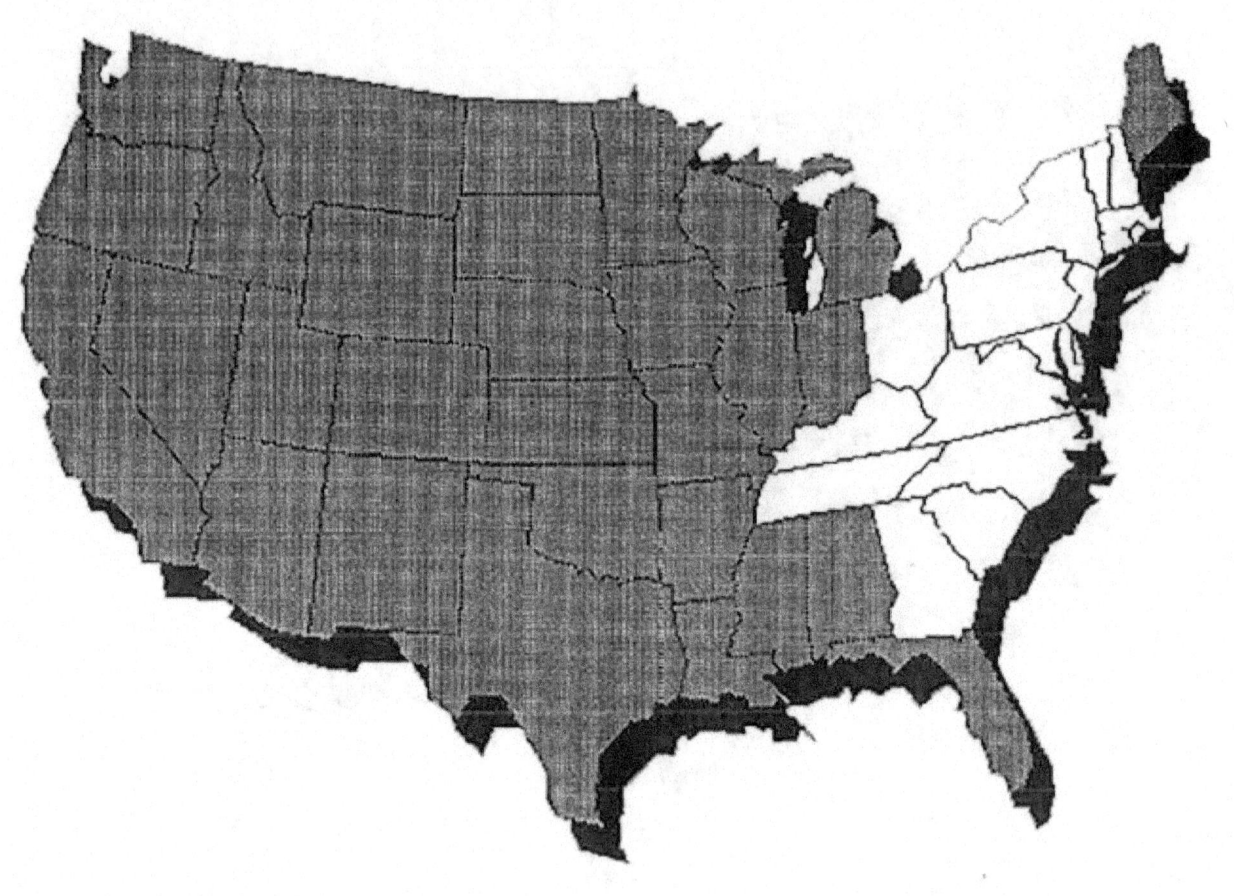

Jefferson's Presidency

Ohio 1803

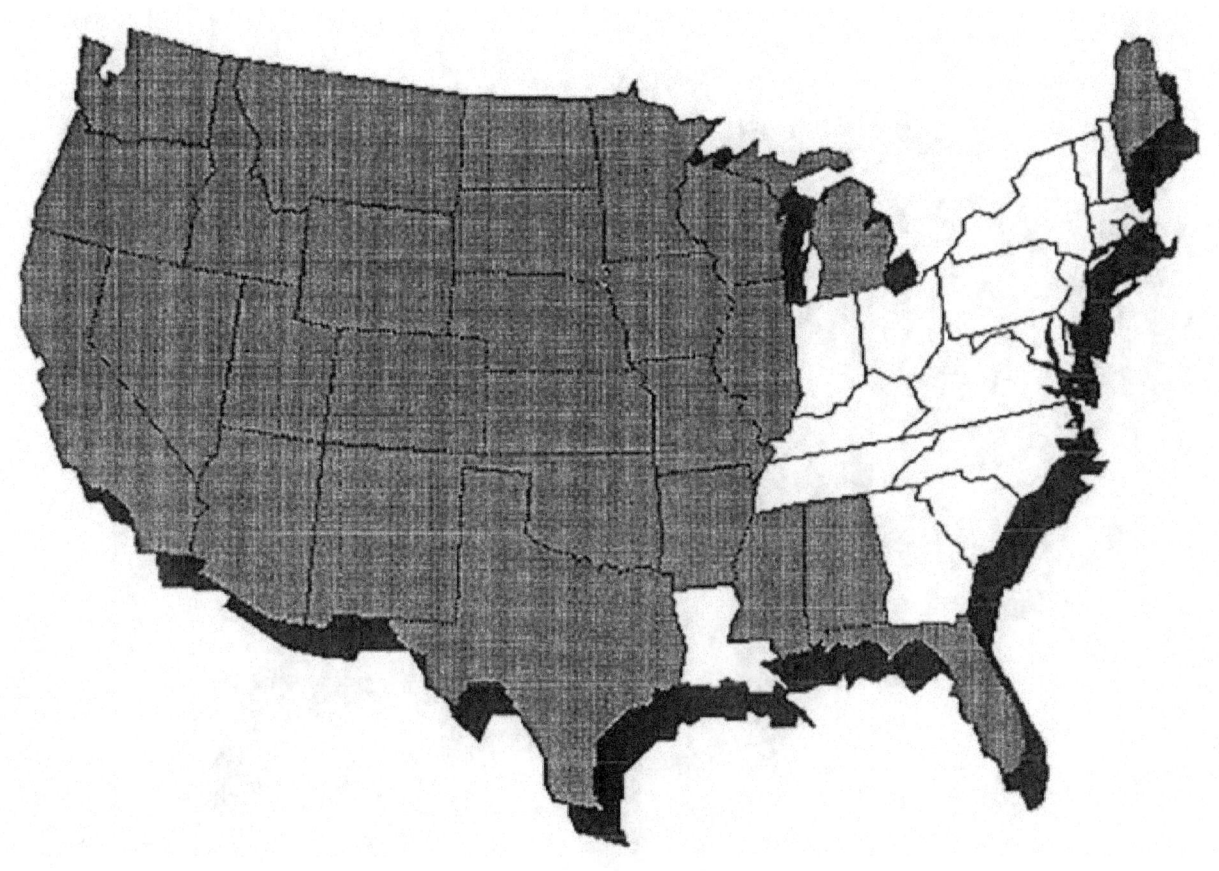

Madison's Presidency

Louisiana 1812
Indiana 1816

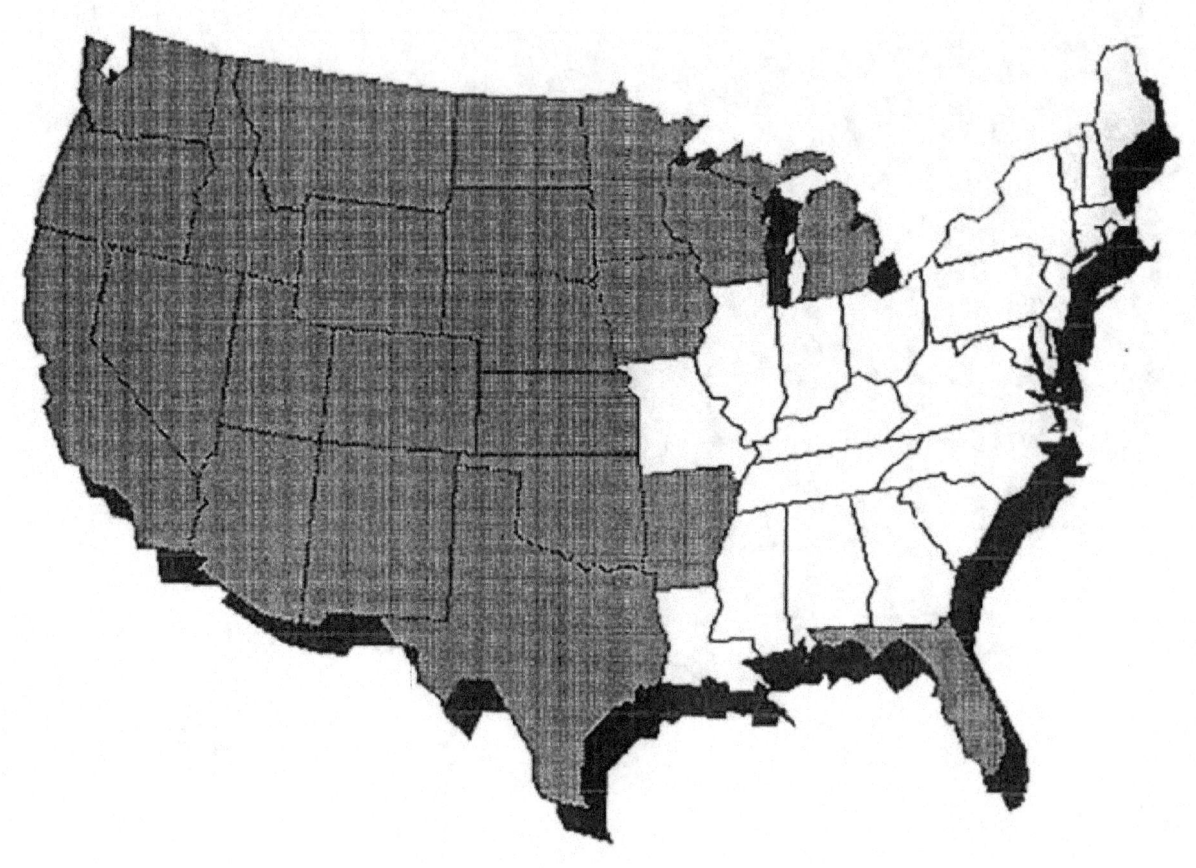

Monroe's Presidency

Mississippi 1817
Illinois 1818
Alabama 1819
Maine 1820
Missouri 1821

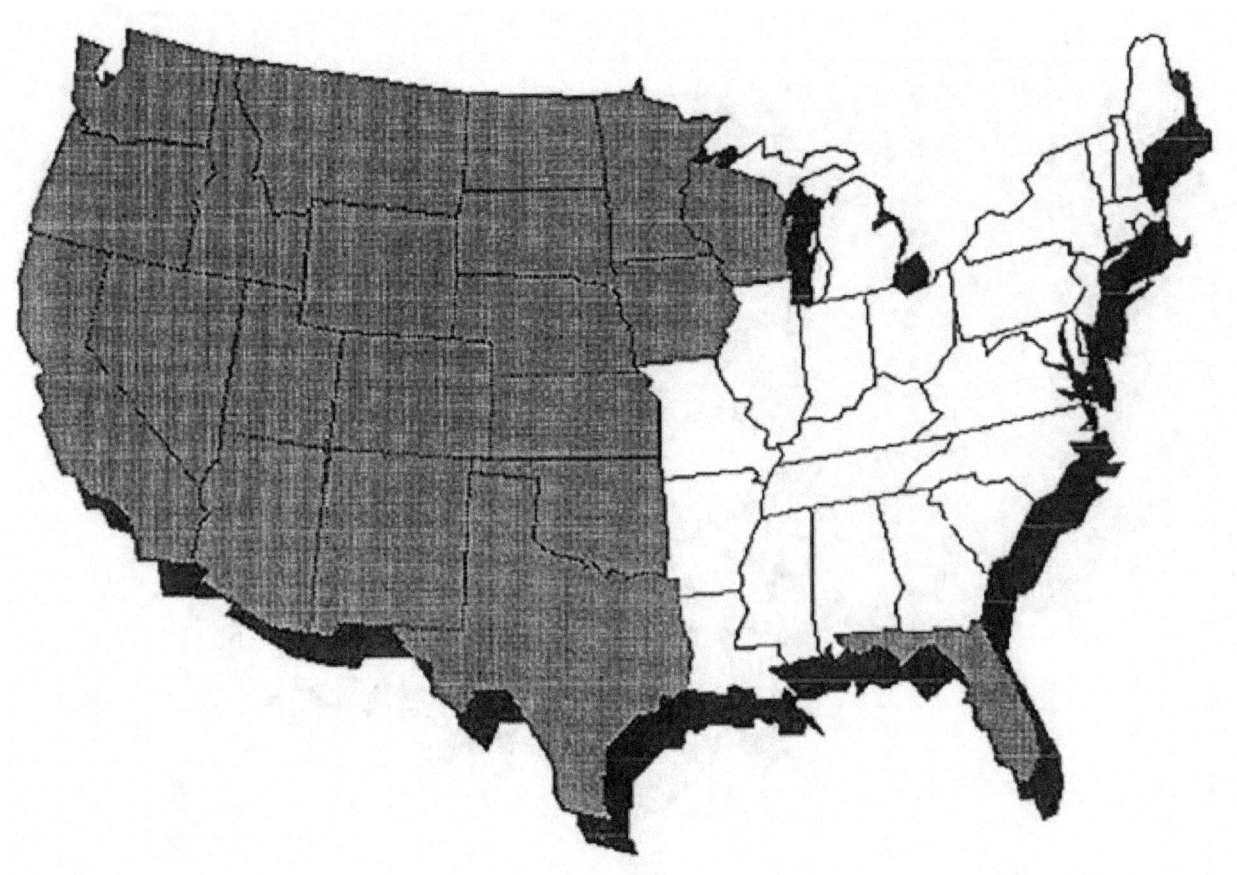

Jackson's Presidency

Arkansas 1836
Michigan 183

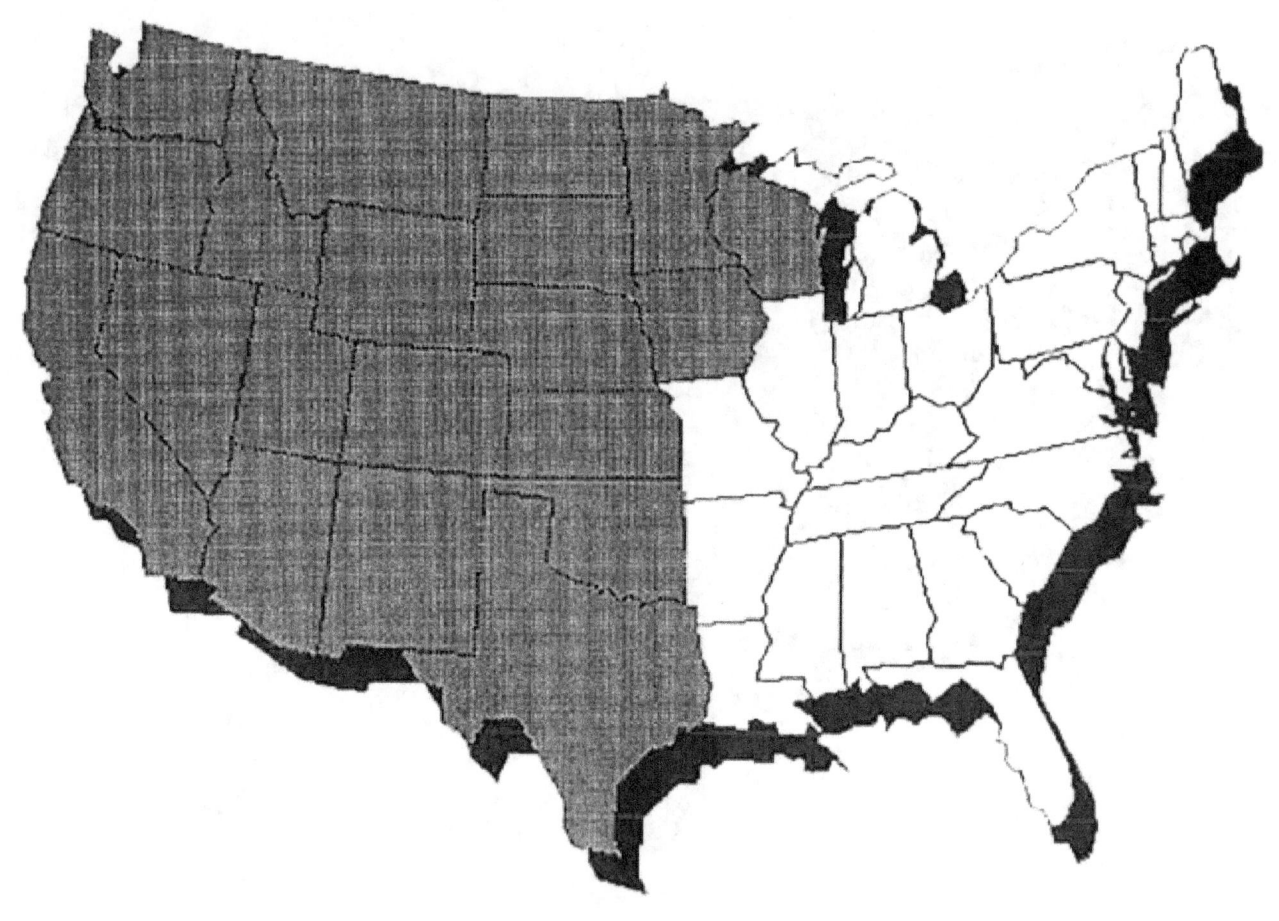

Tyler's Presidency

Florida 1845

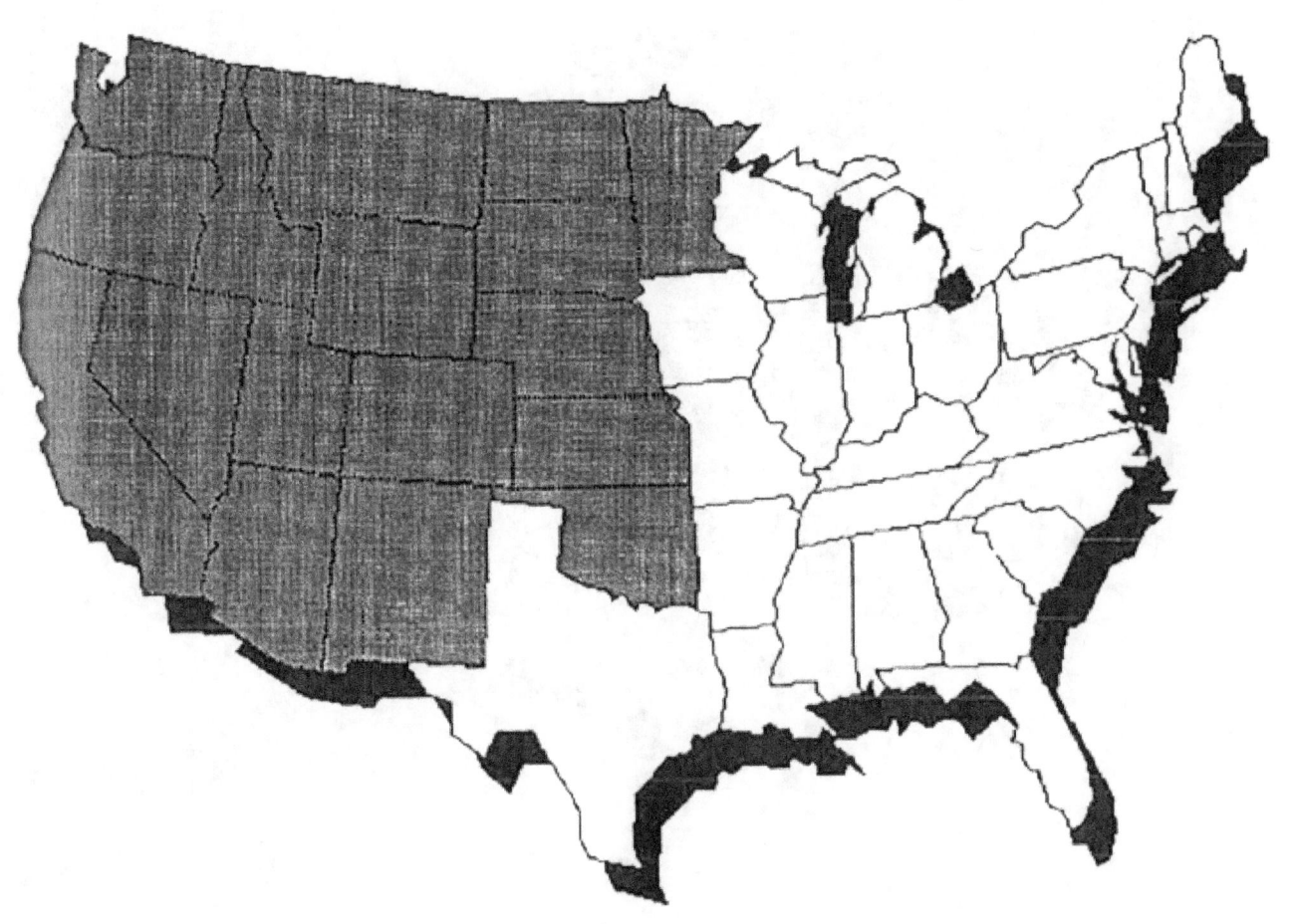

Polk's Presidency

Texas 1845

Iowa 1846

Wisconsin 1848

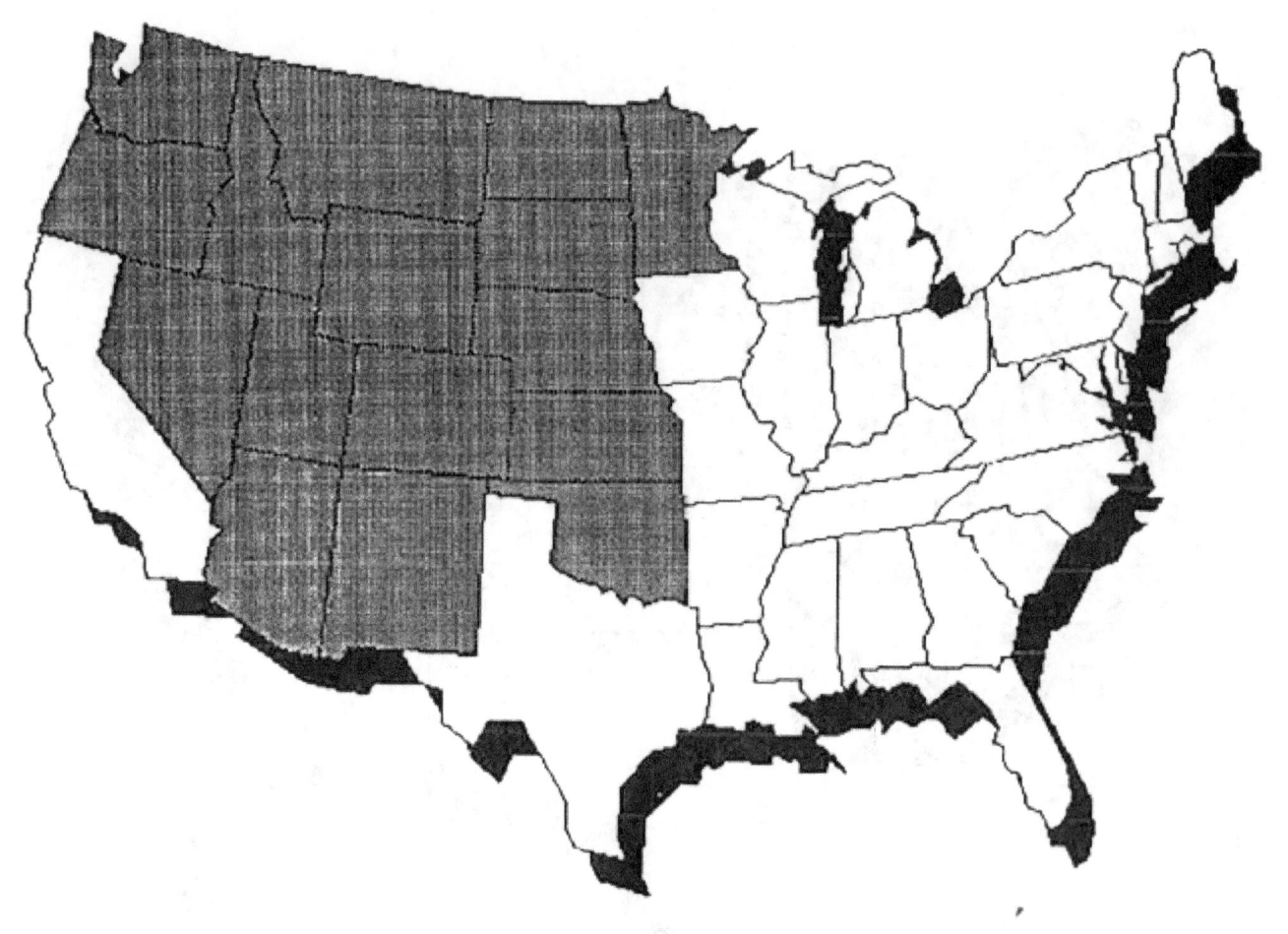

Fillmore's Presidency

California 1850

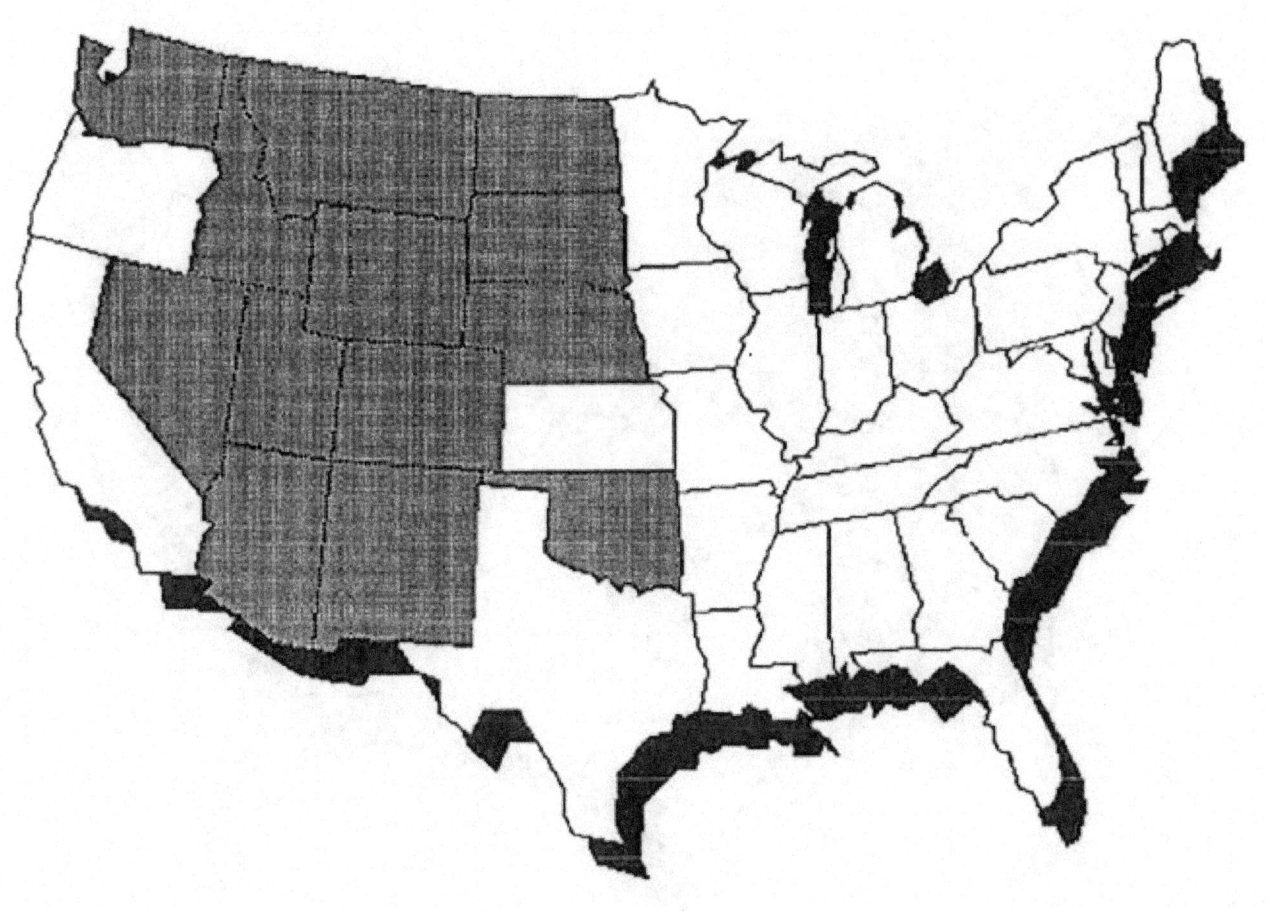

Buchanan's Presidency

Minnesota 1858
Oregon 1859
Kansas 1861

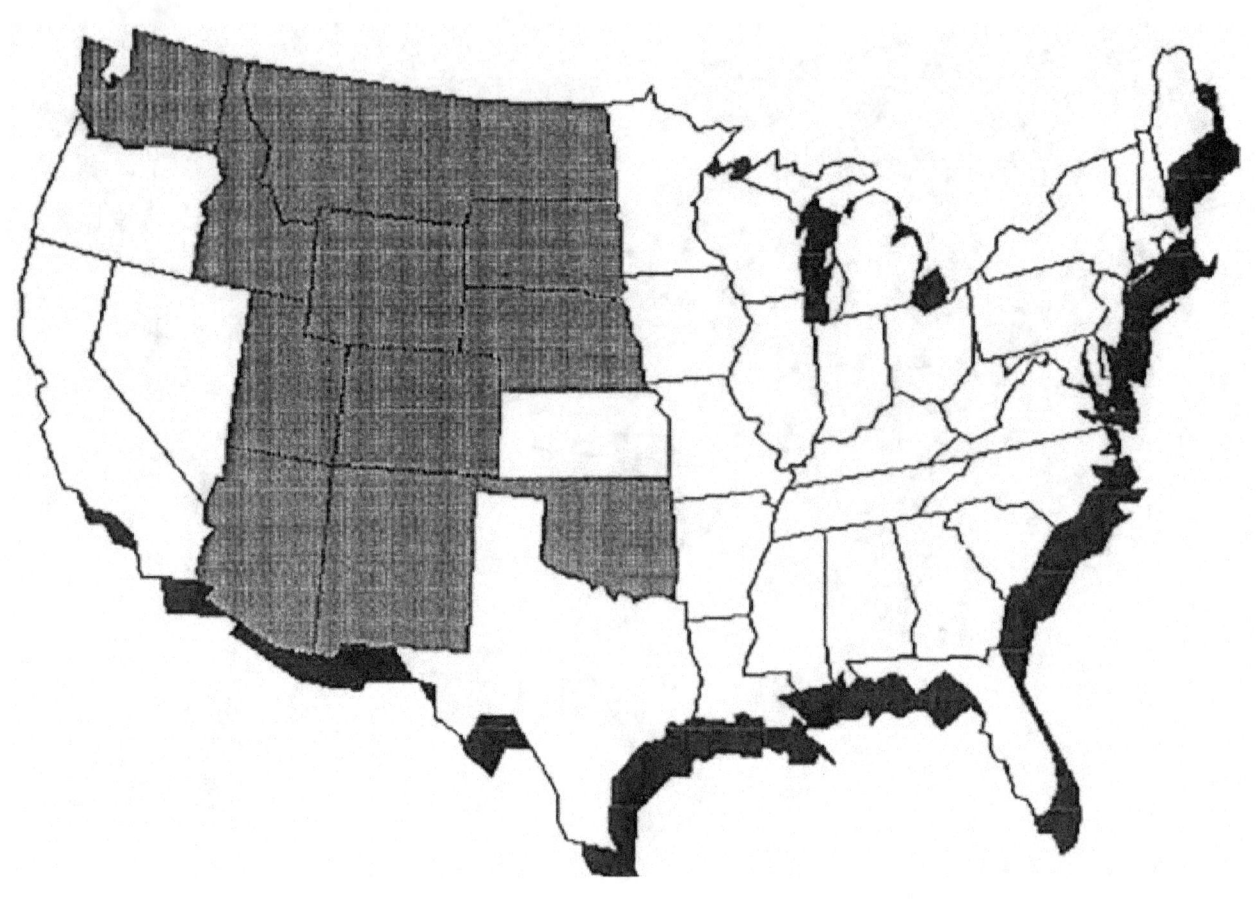

Lincoln's Presidency

West Virginia 1863
Nevada 1864

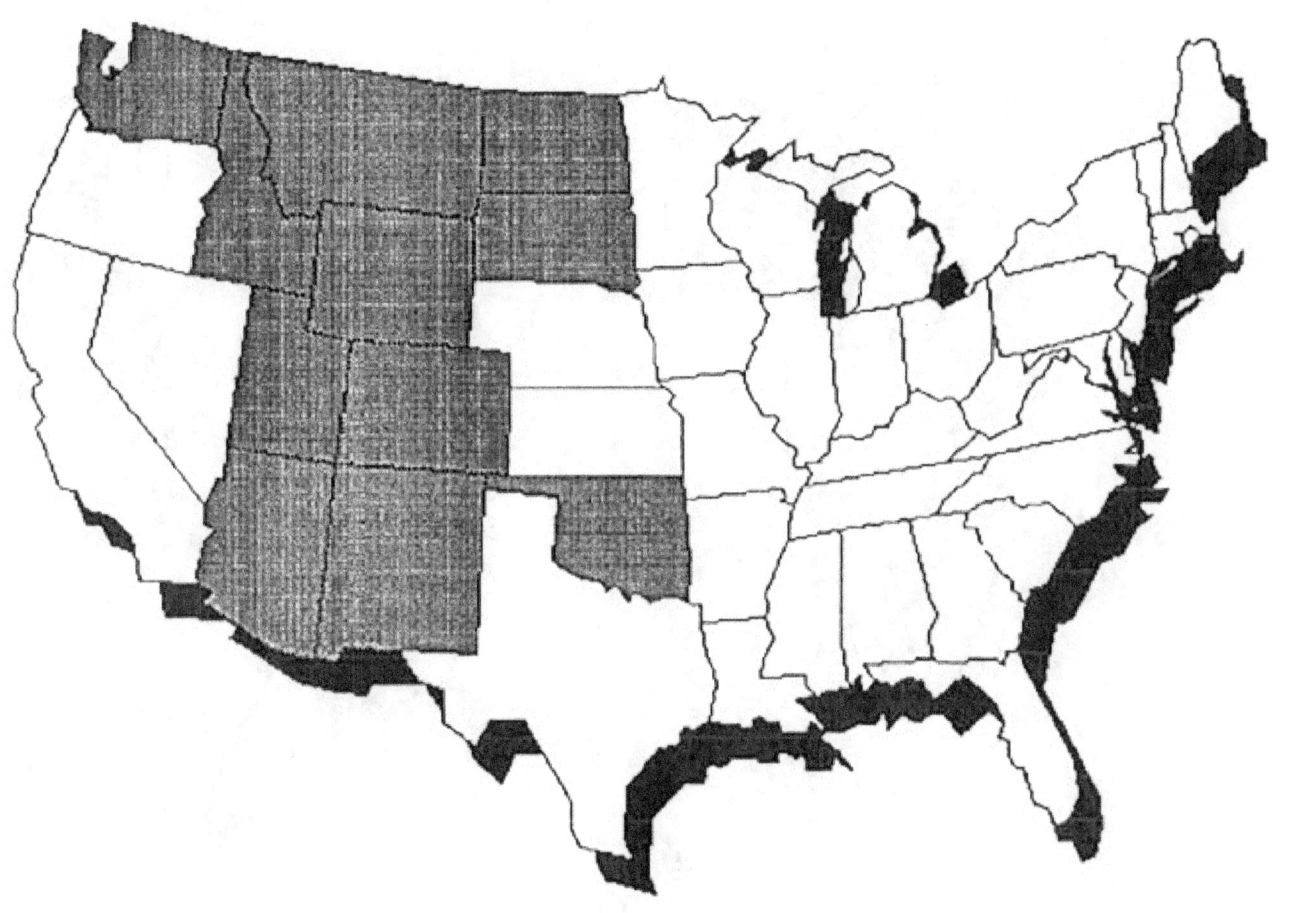

Johnson's Presidency

Nebraska 1867

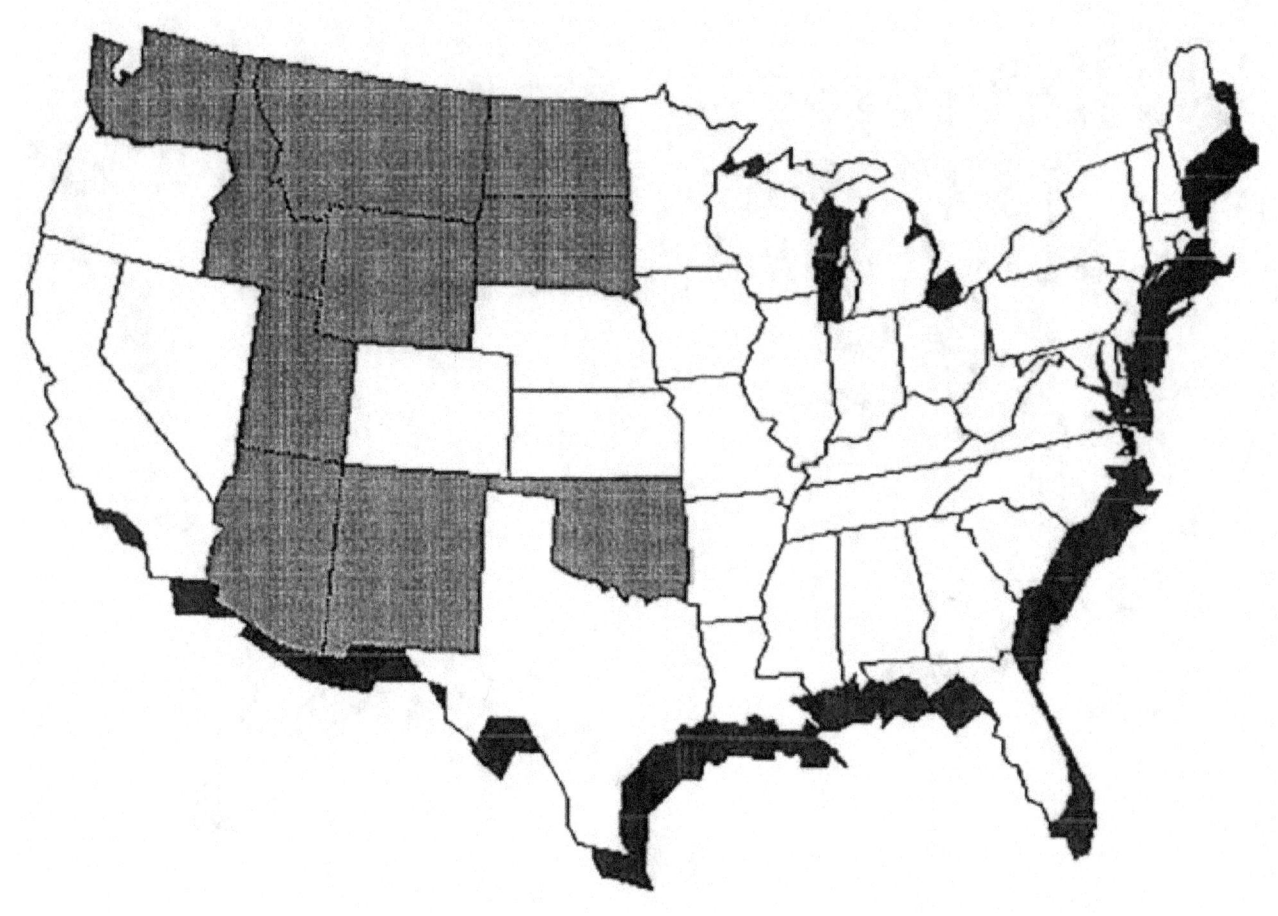

Grant's Presidency

Colorado 1876

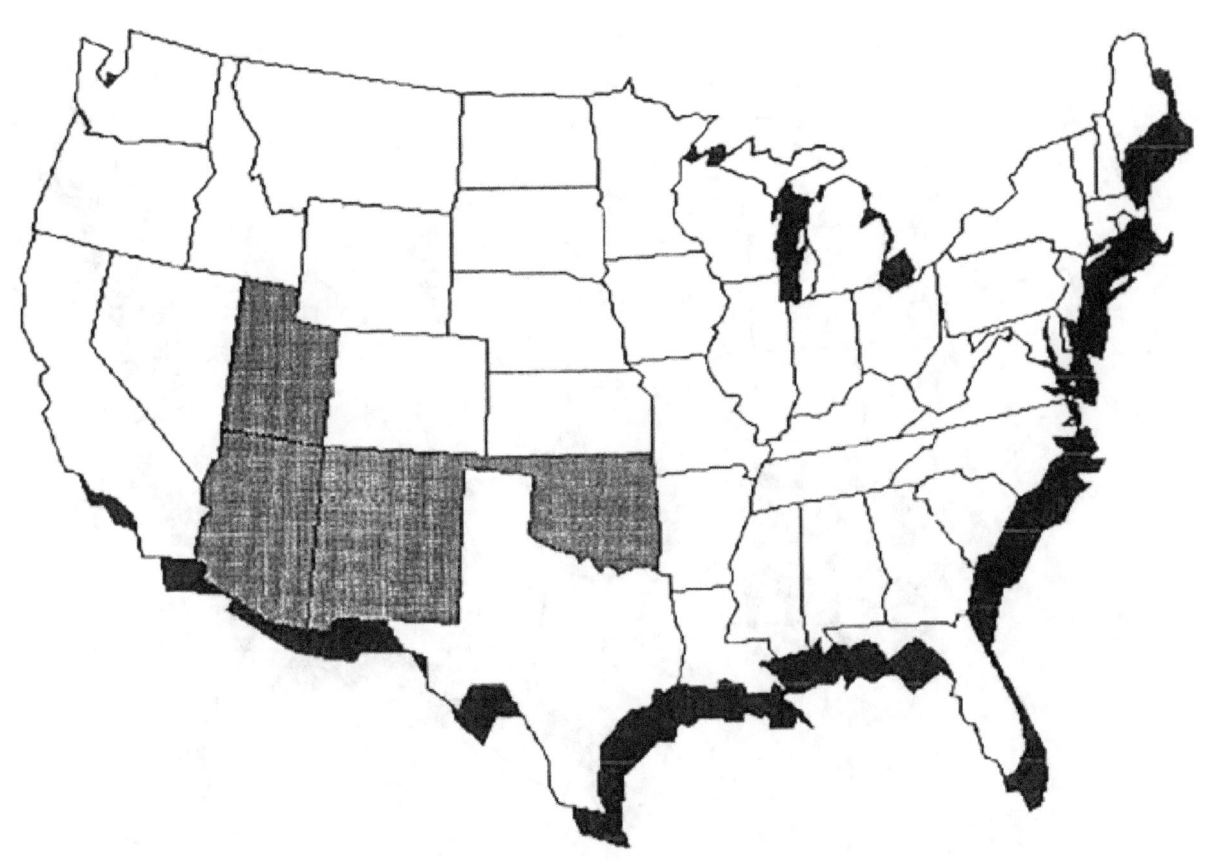

Benjamin Harrison's Presidency

North Dakota 1889
South Dakota 1889
Montana 1889
Washington 1889
Idaho 1890
Wyoming 1890

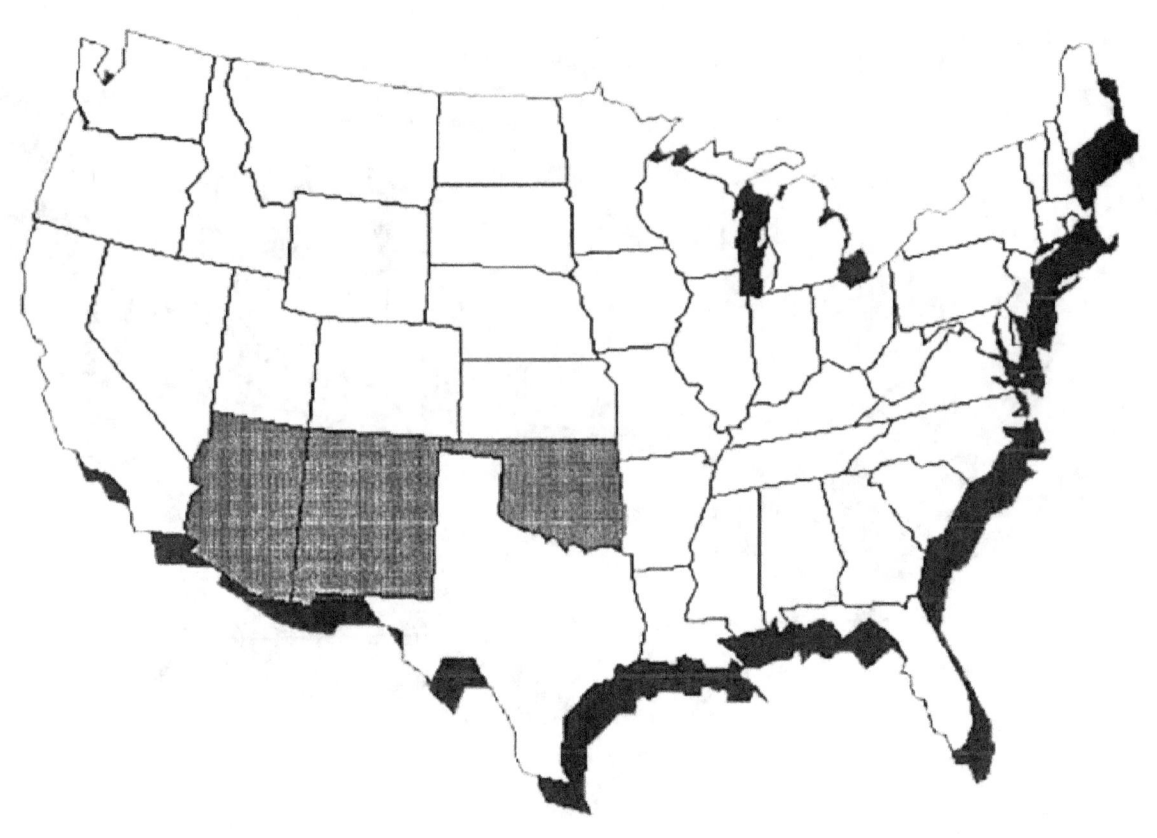

Cleveland's Presidency
(second term)

Utah 1896

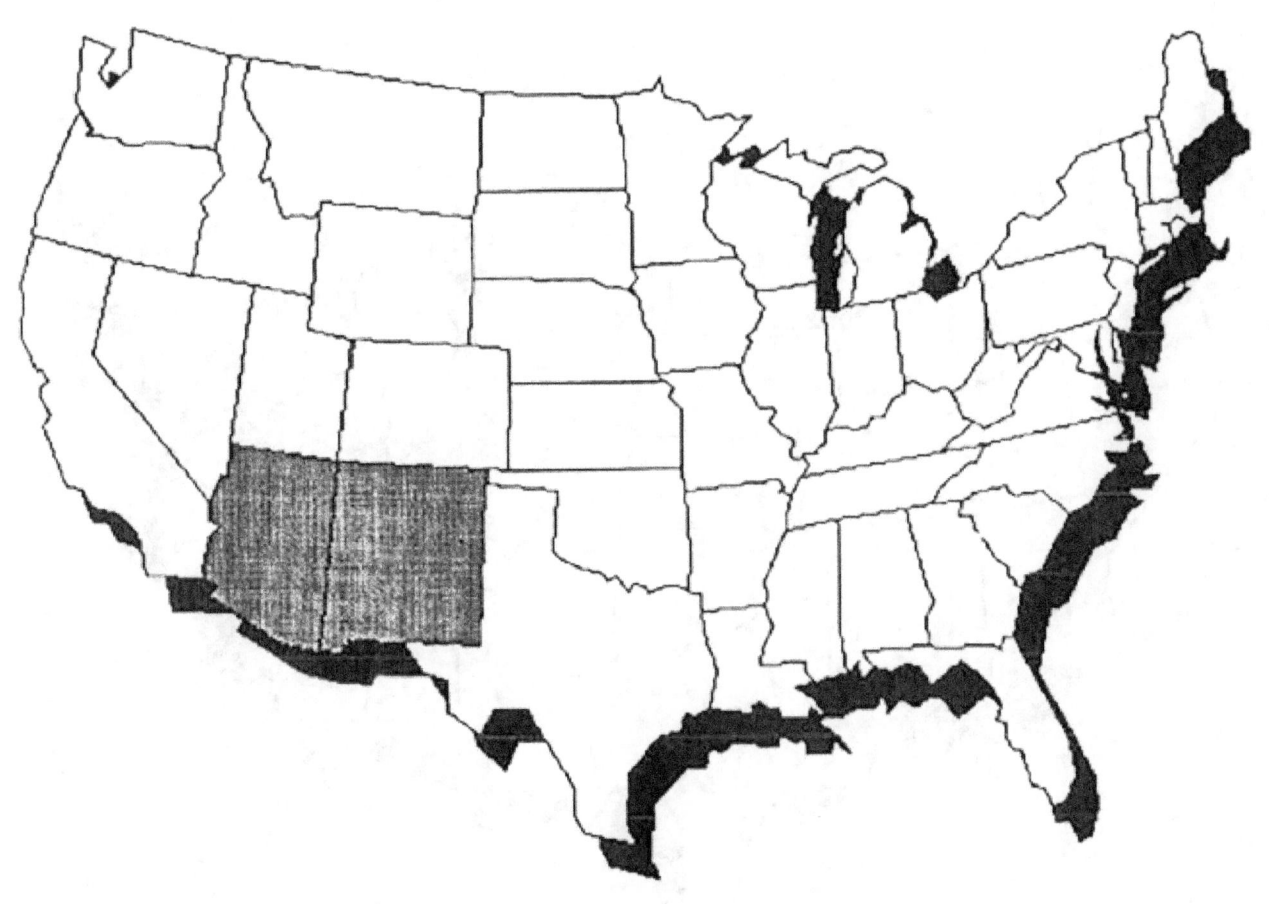

Theodore Roosevelt's Presidency

Oklahoma 1907

Taft's Presidency

New Mexico 1912
Arizona 1912

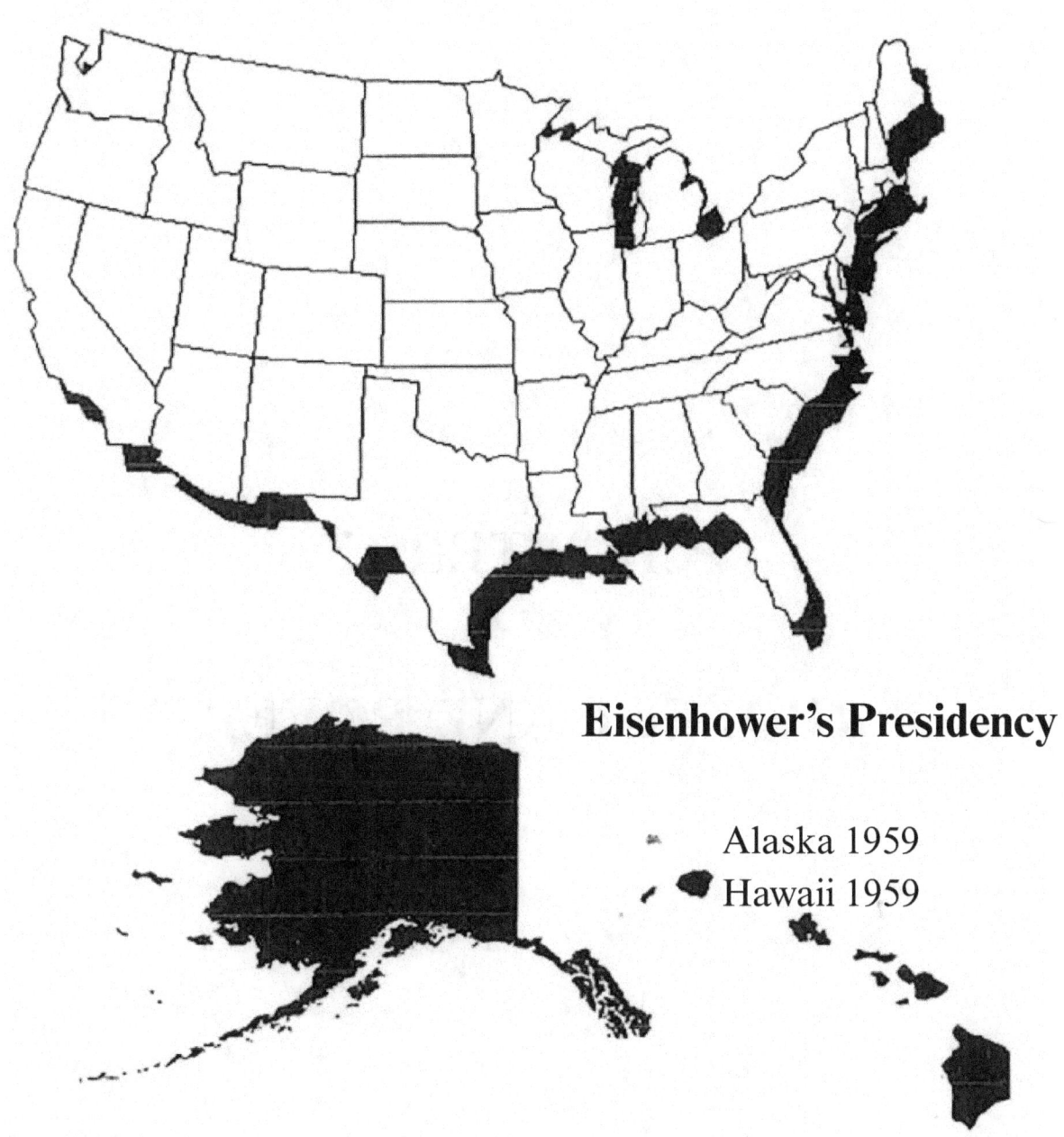

Eisenhower's Presidency

Alaska 1959
Hawaii 1959

CHAPTER 12

PRIVILEGE AND POVERTY

Several presidents grew up in privileged families as children, while many more spent their childhood's in poverty. James Monroe was the son of a prominent and successful Virginia planter. When his father died at age 16, James inherited the entire estate. John Tyler was the son of an aristocratic Virginian family and learned to play the violin well from his father, who was a Virginia governor.

Although born when his family lived in a small log cabin, Franklin Pierce, soon after his birth, moved into a spacious home built by his father in Hillsboro, Lower Village, New Hampshire. As a youngster, Franklin attended private schools and his father was the governor of New Hampshire. When he went to college in Maine, at the age of 15, he met and became a very close friend to Nathaniel Hawthorne, the famous author.

Theodore Roosevelt was the son of a wealthy glass exporter, who left young Teddy, a student at Harvard, $125,000 at his death. His privileged youth included two trips abroad and home tutors due to his sickly health. At age 15, Teddy and his family moved into a newly built mansion on West 57th Street in New York City.

Franklin Delano Roosevelt had a privileged childhood in Hyde Park, New York, along with a summer home and several trips abroad. As a child he had his own pony, and his own sailboat at age 16. Franklin's father taught him that with privilege came responsibility to help those less fortunate.

John Fitzgerald Kennedy was the son of a wealthy Massachusetts family. He attended private schools as a child, spent his summers at Hyannis Port and his winters at Palm Beach, Florida. He, like Teddy Roosevelt, was a sickly child. At age 21, John Fitzgerald Kennedy received a $1,000,000 trust fund that had been established by his father.

George Bush's father was a successful investment banker and George had many privileges as a youngster, including nannies, housekeepers, and chauffeurs. He attended private schools and, like Teddy Roosevelt, was taught by his father that privilege carried the obligation to help others.

As these privileged childhoods led to the presidency, many more that served that office spent their childhoods in poverty. Andrew Jackson was born merely two weeks after his father died, leaving his mother to raise a spirited and often fighting young boy. He lived with a couple different uncles and was at one time apprenticed to a saddler. Although he inherited £350 at age 15 from a grandfather in Ireland, he squandered that money and ended up penniless.

Born in a log cabin in New York, Millard Fillmore spent his youth in a struggling farm family. He was apprenticed to a cloth maker at age 14 and first attended school at age 18.

Abraham Lincoln was born to a poor Kentucky family in a dirt-floor log cabin. Although Lincoln had only a year's worth of formal education and was the son of a man who could neither read nor write, Abe developed a love for reading. He spent his childhood in many chores helping his family in survival. Lincoln has been quoted as saying, in reference to his childhood, "The short and simple annals of the poor".

Andrew Johnson spent his entire childhood in desperate poverty, after his father died when he was only 3. His mother couldn't afford to send her sons to school. He was apprenticed to a tailor as a boy and didn't learn to write until taught by his future wife as a young man.

James Garfield was the last president to be born in a log cabin and spent his childhood in severe poverty after his father died when he was only two. In order to help his family survive, he spent his childhood as a hired hand on farms. Even though he was unable to go to school, he learned to read by three years of age and was a voracious reader as a youngster.

Orphaned by age nine, Herbert Hoover had at age six been sent to live with relatives, after his father's death, to help ease the financial burden on his mother. After his mother's death, he was sent from relative to relative. Hoover went from rags to riches, becoming a millionaire by age 40. He said at the time of accepting the presidential nomination in 1928, approximately a year and a half before the Great Depression began, "We in America today are nearer to the final triumph over poverty than ever before in the history of any land. The poorhouse is vanishing from among us. We have not yet reached that goal, but given a chance to go forward with the policies of the last eight years, and we shall soon, with the help of God, be in sight of the day when poverty shall be banished from this nation."

Shortly after his birth in a rented room near the railroad tracks in Denison, Texas, Dwight Eisenhower's family moved to Kansas. There his father went bankrupt, plummeting the family into severe poverty. Young Ike was teased for wearing hand-me-downs, particularly his mother's shoes. He helped contribute to the family's survival by selling vegetables from the family garden, hauling ice, and shoveling coal.

Lyndon Johnson helped to ease the hardship his family endured in Johnson City, Texas by being a hired hand on local farms, being a shoe shine boy, and trapping and selling animal skins. He was born in a three-room farmhouse.

Richard Nixon was born to an economically struggling family in Loma Linda, California. His father failed at growing lemons and they returned to Whittier, where young Richard helped with the delivery of produce for the Nixon market.

Ronald Reagan was born in a rental apartment above a bakery in Tampico, Illinois. When he was two years old, he lived on the south side of Chicago. By age nine the family settled in Dixon, where Ron grew up in a lower-middle-class environment. He remembers as a child sorting potatoes in a hot, stuffy boxcar.

Donald Trump becomes the first billionaire president. His father, Fred Trump, was in construction and Donald had an affluent upbringing. There is much disagreement of the amount of his vast wealth.

LEVEL VI PRESIDENTIAL QUIZ

1. Prior to President Clinton, name the only three presidents during the 1900s to serve two full consecutive terms.

2. Name the five presidents in the 1800s who served two consecutive full terms.

3. Although there has only been one decade in which no president has been born, there have been four decades in which no U.S. President has died. Name those 4 decades.

4. Name the eight presidents born in Virginia.

5. Name seven presidents born in Ohio.

6. Name the president who admitted, during the presidential campaign, to fathering an illegitimate child.

7. How many presidents have had their wife die during their lifetime?

8. Name the presidents who were widowers.

9. Name three presidents who were married in their 40s.

10. Name the president whose wife's first name was Letitia.

11. Name the president whose wife's name was Lucretia.

12. Name the president whose wife's name was Claudia.

13. Name the president whose wife's name was Thelma.

14. Name the six presidents whose first name was James.

15. Who was president on April 5th, 1841?

16. Other than January or March, name the month in which four presidents have become president. Name the four presidents.

17. One president was sworn into office in July and one president was inaugurated in November. Name the two respective presidents.

18. Two presidents assumed their duties in August. Name them.

19. Two presidents were sworn in in September. Name them.

20. Name four presidents who were governors of New York.

21. Name the three presidents who were widowed while in office.

22. Name the six wives of presidents who never became first ladies because they died or divorced before their husband served in the office.

23. Name six presidents who had no children.

24. Who's the only president to have six states admitted to the Union during his presidency, and name the six states?

25. Name the four presidents born in February.

26. Name the only president born in June.

27. Name the two presidents married to an Abigail.

28. Name the president during the War of 1812.

29. Name the president during the Mexican War.

30. Name the president during the Spanish-American War.

31. Name the two presidents during the Korean War.

32. Name the president during the Gulf War.

33. Name four presidents born in January.

34. Name the president born in Virginia the day after George Washington's father died in Virginia.

35. Name the only president born on July 4th.

36. Name five presidents born in August.

37. Who was the only president born in September?

38. Which president was married to Lucy and was governor of Ohio?

39. Which president married Julia after his first wife died?

40. Name two presidents that married a woman named Edith after their first wife died.

41. Who was president when Arkansas and Michigan were admitted to the Union?

42. Who was president when Oklahoma was admitted to the Union?

43. Ten presidents were married between the ages of 20 to 24, and twentythree were married at ages 25 to30. Name the nine who were married either younger than 20 or older than 30.

44. Name the month in which no president has ever died.

45. More presidents have died in July than in any other month: three died on July 4th, and one died on July 9th, having become ill on July 4th. Name the other three to have died in July.

46. Name the president who married for the first time at the oldest age.

47. Fifteen presidents died on days ending in a 4 or divisible by 4. Name them.

48. Name the only presidents born in each of the following states: South Carolina, New Hampshire, Pennsylvania, Kentucky, New Jersey, Iowa, Mississippi, California, Nebraska, Georgia, Illinois, Arkansas, and Connecticut.

49. Name two presidents born in North Carolina.

50. Name two presidents born in Vermont.

51. Name two presidents born in Texas.

52. Name eight presidents who had two children.

53. Name the two presidents who had only one child.

54. Name seven presidents who were economically privileged during their childhood.

55. Which president joined the confederacy after serving his term as president?

56. Which president was a descendant of someone who was on the Mayflower?

57. Who was the first First Lady with a college degree?

58. Who was the first left-handed president?

59. Name two presidents whose middle name was that of another president.

60. Name the only president to die in office who was not elected in the "every- twenty-years" cycle from Harrison 1840 to Kennedy in 1960.

CHAPTER 13

NAMES

Seventeen presidents did not have middle names. They were Washington, Adams, Jefferson, Madison, Monroe, Jackson, Van Buren, Tyler, Taylor, Fillmore, Pierce, Buchanan, Lincoln, Andrew Johnson, Benjamin Harrison, McKinley, and Theodore Roosevelt.

Five presidents did not use their given first names. Ulysses S. Grant was named Hiram Ulysses Grant at birth; an error at West Point had his name as Ulysses Simpson and he never bothered to correct it. Stephen

Grover Cleveland dropped Stephen and went by Grover Cleveland. Thomas Woodrow Wilson dropped Thomas and went by Woodrow. John Calvin Coolidge dropped John and went by Calvin. Dwight Eisenhower was born David Dwight and later switched his first and second name to become Dwight David. Two presidents have middle names, which are also the last name of former presidents. They are: Ronald Wilson Reagan and William Jefferson Clinton.

Two presidents had different last names at birth. President Ford was born Leslie Lynch King, Jr. and, after his mother divorced his father and remarried Gerald Rudolph Ford, he was renamed Gerald Rudolph Ford. President Clinton was born William Jefferson Blythe IV. His father died before he was born and, when his mother married Mr. Clinton, his name was changed to William Jefferson Clinton. Harry Truman's middle name is simply "S", rather than an initial standing for something. His parents gave him the middle "S" after his two grandparents, Solomon Young and Anderson Shippe Truman.

There were two presidents named Adams: father and son, John and John Quincy, respectively. There were two presidents named Harrison: William Henry and grandson Benjamin. There were two presidents named Johnson, Andrew and Lyndon, and they were not related. There were two presidents named Roosevelt, Theodore and Franklin, and they were fifth cousins. A second father and son served as presidents when George W. Bush took office. The eldest President Bush is the only president with two middle names; Herbert Walker.

Three presidents were named George: Washington and the two Bushes. Five presidents were named John: Adams, Quincy Adams, Tyler, John Calvin Coolidge, and Kennedy. Two presidents were named Thomas: Thomas Jefferson and Thomas Woodrow Wilson. Six presidents were named James: Madison, Monroe, Polk, Buchanan, Garfield, and Carter. Two presidents were named Andrew: Jackson and Johnson. Four presidents were named William: Harrison, McKinley, Taft, and Clinton. Two presidents were named Franklin: Pierce and Roosevelt.

Eight first ladies went by names other than their given name. Seven of those were consecutive first ladies. Margaret Taylor went by Peggy in the middle of the 19th Century. The seven consecutive first ladies were Elizabeth Truman, who went by Bess; Marie Eisenhower, who went by Mamie; Jacqueline Kennedy, who went by Jackie; Claudia Johnson, who went by Lady Bird; Thelma Nixon, who went by Pat; Elizabeth Ford, who went by Betty; and Eleanor Rosalyn Carter, who went by Rosalyn.

There have been two wives of presidents named Martha: Washington, who was the first First Lady, and Jefferson, who died before Thomas Jefferson was president. Two presidential wives were named Abigail: John Adam's wife and Millard Fillmore's. Two presidents' wives named Ellen died, leaving the president a widower: Ellen Arthur and Ellen Wilson. There were four Elizabeth's or Eliza's: Monroe, Johnson, Truman, and Ford. Two presidents had second wives named Edith: Theodore Roosevelt and Wilson.

CHAPTER 14

RELATIVES

Almost half of all presidents through George W. Bush (twenty of the forty five presidents) were related to another president. James Monroe and Richard Nixon were both descendants of Britain's King Edward III, although their relationship to each other is not exactly determined.

John Adams was the father of President John Quincy Adams. Coincidentally, John Adams married his third cousin, making John Quincy Adams a third cousin, once removed, of his own mother.

William Henry Harrison was the grandfather of President Benjamin Harrison. President Tyler was the great uncle of Harry Truman.

Besides the distant relationship that President Nixon had to President Monroe, Richard Nixon was also the seventh cousin, twice removed, of William Howard Taft. Nixon was also the eighth cousin, once removed, of Herbert Hoover. Both President George Washington and Theodore Roosevelt were related to Winston Churchill, Washington being his eighth cousin, six times removed, and Roosevelt being Churchill's seventh cousin, once removed. George Washington was a half-first cousin, twice removed, of James Madison, and James Madison was a second cousin of Zachary Taylor. Zachary Taylor was a descendant of William Brewster, a pilgrim who sailed on the Mayflower. Zachary Taylor was also a fourth cousin, three times removed, of Theodore Roosevelt and a fourth cousin, three times removed, of Franklin Delano Roosevelt. Theodore Roosevelt was a third cousin, twice removed, of Martin Van Buren and a fifth cousin of Franklin Delano Roosevelt. Franklin Roosevelt's wife, Eleanor, was his fifth cousin, once removed, as Eleanor was Theodore Roosevelt's niece. Franklin Roosevelt was also a fourth cousin, once removed, of Ulysses S. Grant, and Ulysses S. Grant was a sixth cousin, once removed, of Grover Cleveland.

William Henry Harrison was a descendant of King Henry III of England and George Washington was a second cousin, seven times removed, of Queen Elizabeth II of England.

George Herbert Walker Bush and son George Walker Bush made Barbara the second woman to be wife and mother of U.S. presidents. Barbara Bush is the first woman to see her husband and son as president. Abigail Adams died before her son was president.

APPENDIX

Chronological list of U.S. Presidents.

1. George Washington
2. John Adams
3. Thomas Jefferson
4. James Madison
5. James Monroe
6. John Quincy Adams
7. Andrew Jackson
8. Martin Van Buren
9. William Henry Harrison
10. John Tyler
11. James Knox Polk
12. Zachary Taylor
13. Millard Fillmore
14. Franklin Pierce
15. James Buchanan
16. Abraham Lincoln
17. Andrew Johnson
18. Ulysses Simpson Grant
19. Rutherford Birchard Hayes
20. James Abram Garfield
21. Chester Alan Arthur
22. Steven Grover Cleveland
23. Benjamin Harrison
24. Steven Grover Cleveland
25. William McKinley
26. Theodore Roosevelt

27. William Howard Taft

28. Thomas Woodrow Wilson

29. Warren Gamaliel Harding

30. John Calvin Coolidge

31. Herbert Clark Hoover

32. Franklin Delano Roosevelt

33. Harry S Truman

34. Dwight David Eisenhower

35. John Fitzgerald Kennedy

36. Lyndon Baines Johnson

37. Richard Milhouse Nixon
38. Gerald Rudolph Ford

39. James Earl Carter

40. Ronald Wilson Reagan

41. George Herbert Walker Bush

42. William Jefferson Clinton

43. George Walker Bush

44. Barack Hussein Obama

45. Donald John Trump

46. Joseph R. Biden

47. Donald J. Trump

48.

49.

50.

CALENDARS

JANUARY

1	2	3	4	5	6	7
Jefferson married Martha 1772 Polk married Sarah, 1824			Reagan's daughter, Maureen, born 1941	Coolidge died 1933	T. Roosevelt died 1919 Washington married Martha, 1759 Bush married Barbara, 1945 Eric Trump born 1984	Fillmore born 1800
8	**9** Nixon born 1913	**10**	**11**	**12** Ellen Arthur died 1880	**13**	**14**
15	**16** Van Buren's son, Smith, born 1817	**17** Michelle Obama born 1964 Hayes died 1893 Jackson married Rachel, 1794 (2ᵈ time)	**18** Tyler died 1862	**19**	**20** Inauguration Day	**21**
22 L.B. Johnson died 1973 Bush's son, Neil born, 1955 Trump Married Melania 2005	**23**	**24** Reagan married Jane, 1940	**25** McKinley married Ida, 1871 McKinley's daughter, Katherine, born 1872	**26**	**27** Taylor's son, Richard born 1826	**28**
29 McKinley born 1843	**30** FDR born 1882	**31**				

FEBUARY

1	2	3	4	5	6	7
	Pierce's son, Franklin, born 1836	Wilsom died 1924		Filmore married Abigail, 1826	Reagan born 1911	
8 Hayes' son, Scott, born 1871	**9** William Henry Harrison born 1773	**10** Fillmore married Carolyn, 1858 Hoover married Lou, 1899	**11** Bush's son, John Born 1953	**12** Lincoln born 1809 Roosevelt's daughter, Alice born 1884	**13**	**14** Alice Roosevelt died 1884
15	**16** Monroe married Elizabeth, 1786	**17** Truman's daughter, Mary Margaret, born 1924	**18** Van Buren's son John born 1810	**19** Andrew Johnson's son, Charles, born 1830	**20**	**21** Van Buren married Hannah 1807
22 Washington born 1732	**23** John Quincy Adams died 1848	**24**	**25**	**26**	**27** Clinton's daughter, Chelsea, born 1980	**28**
29						

MARCH

1	2	3	4	5	6	7
	Pierce's son, Franklin, born 1836	Wilsom died 1924		Filmore married Abigail, 1826	Reagan born 1911	
8	9	10	11	12	13	14
Hayes' son, Scott, born 1871	William Henry Harrison born 1773	Fillmore married Carolyn, 1858 Hoover married Lou, 1899	Bush's son, John Born 1953	Lincoln born 1809 Roosevelt's daughter, Alice born 1884		Alice Roosevelt died 1884
15	16	17	18	19	20	21
	Monroe married Elizabeth, 1786	Truman's daughter, Mary Margaret, born 1924	Van Buren's son John born 1810	Andrew Johnson's son, Charles, born 1830		Van Buren married Hannah 1807
22	23	24	25	26	27	28
Washington born 1732	John Quincy Adams died 1848				Clinton's daughter, Chelsea, born 1980	
29						

APRIL

1	2	3	4	5	6	7
		Jefferson's daughter, Jane, born 1774	William Henry Harrison died 1841		Tyler assumed presidency, 1841 Benjamin Harrison married Mary, 1896	Tyler's son, John, born 1848
8	9	10	11	12	13	14
	Taylor's daughter, Anne, born 1811			F.D. Roosevelt died 1945 Truman takes over as president, 1945	Jefferson born 1743	Lincoln shot 1865
15	16	17	18	19	20	21
Lincoln died 1865 Andrew Johnson became president, 1865					Taylor's daughter, Mary, born 1824	
22	23	24	25	26	27	28
Nixon died 1994	Buchanan born 1791		Fillmore's son, Millard, born 1828	Melania Trump born 1970	Grant born 1822	Monroe born 1758
29	30	31				
	Washinton became president, 1789 Wilson's daughter born 1886					

MAY

1	2	3 F.D. Roosevelt's daughter, Anna born 1906	4	5	6	7
8 Truman born 1884	9	10	11 Tyler's daughter, Letitia, born 1821	12	13	14
15	16	17 Andrew Johnson married Eliza, 1827	18	19 Ford's son, Steven, born 1956	20 Reagan's son, Ronald, born 1958	21
22	23	24	25	26	27	28 Jefferson's unnamed son born 1777
29 Kennedy born 1917	30 Grant's son, Frederick, born 1850	31				

JUNE

1	2	3	4	5	6	7
Buchanan died 1868	Cleveland married Frances, 1886			Reagan died 2004		
8	**9**	**10**	**11**	**12**	**13**	**14**
Jackson died 1845		Sasha Obama born 2001		Bush born 1924		Donald Trump born 1946
15	**16**	**17**	**18**	**19**	**20**	**21**
Polk died 1849		Joe and Jill Biden married 1977		Taft married Helen 1886	Tyler's daughter, Pearl, born 1860	Taylor married Peggy, 1810 Nixon married Pat, 1940
22	**23**	**24**	**25**	**26**	**27**	**28**
		Cleveland died 1908 Wilson married Ellen, 1885		Tyler married Julia, 1844		Madison died 1836 Truman married Bess, 1919
29	**30**	**31**				

JULY

1	2	3	4	5	6	7
Eisenhower married Mamie, 1916	Garfield shot, 1881 L.B. Johnson's daughter, Lucy, born 1947	Garfield's daughter, Eliza, born 1860 Carter's son, John, born 1947	Malia Obama born 1998 Coolidge born 1872 Jefferson died 1826 Adams died 1826 Monroe died 1831	Nixon's daughter, Julie born 1948	George W. Bush born 1946 Ford's daughter, Susan, born 1957	Carter married Rosalyn, 1946
8	9	10	11	12	13	14
Harding married Florence, 1891	Taylor died 1850	Fillmore sworn in 1850	John Quincy Adams born 1767	Tyler's son, David, born 1846		Ford born 1913
15	16	17	18	19	20	21
		Hoover's son, Allan, born 1907	Cleveland's son, Francis, born 1903			
22	23	24	25	26	27	28
Grant's son, Ulysses, born 1852	Grant died 1885	Van Buren died 1862	Arthur's son, Chester, born 1864	John Quincy Adams married Louisa, 1797	Taylor's daughter, Margaret, born 1819	
29	30	31				
		Andrew Johnson died 1875				

AUGUST

1	2	3	4	5	6	7
Jefferson' daughter, Mary, born 1778	Harding died 1923	Coolidge assumed presidency, 1923	Obama born 1961 Hoover's son, Herbert, born 1903	Andrew Johnson's son, Andrew, born 1852	First Lady Ellen Wilson died 1914	Kennedy's son, Patrick, born 1963
8	**9**	**10**	**11**	**12**	**13**	**14**
Nixon announced his resignation, 1974	Ford became president, 1974	Hoover born 1874		Benjamin Harrison's son, Russell, born 1854	Theodore Roosevelt's daughter, Ethel, born 1891	
15	**16**	**17**	**18**	**19**	**20**	**21**
	Taylor's daughter, Octavia, born 1816	F.D. Roosevelt's son, FDR, Jr., born 1914	John Quincy Adam's son, Charles, born 1807 Carter's son, Donnel, born 1952 Bush's daughter, Dorothy, born 1959	Clinton born 1946	Benjamin Harrison born 1833	
22	**23**	**24**	**25**	**26**	**27**	**28**
Grant married Julia, 1848					L.B. Johnson born 1908	Wilson's son, Jessie, born 1887
29	**30**	**31**				

SEPTEMBER

1	2	3	4	5	6	7
	Hayes' daughter, Fanny, born 1867	William Henry Harrison's son, William Henry, born 1802			Martha Jefferson died, 1782 McKinley shot 1901	Coolidge's son, John, born 1906
8 Taft's son, Robert, born 1889	**9** Tyler's son, Robert, born 1816	**10** First Lady Letitia Tyler died 1842	**11**	**12** Kennedy married Jacqueline, 1953	**13** T. Roosevelt's son, Theodore, born 1887	**14** McKinley died, 1901 Theodore Roosevelt sworn in 1901
15 Taft born 1857 Madison married Dolley, 1794	**16**	**17**	**18**	**19** Garfield died, 1881	**20** Arthur ascends to presidency, 1881	**21**
22 Rachel Jackson died, 1828	**23** F.D. Roosevelt's son, Elliot, born 1910	**24** Eisenhower's son, Dwight, born 1917	**25**	**26**	**27** Jefferson's daughter, Martha, born 1772	**28**
29 William Henry Harrison's daughter, Elizabeth, born 1796	**30**	**31**				

OCTOBER

1	2	3	4	5	6	7
Carter born 1924		Cleveland's daughter, Ruth, born 1891	Hayes born, 1822 Coolidge married Grace, 1905	Arthur born 1830		
8	**9**	**10**	**11**	**12**	**13**	**14**
Pierce died 1869		T. Roosevelt's son Kermit, born 1889	Clinton married Hillary, 1975		Tiffany Trump born 1993	Eisenhower born, 1890
15	**16**	**17**	**18**	**19**	**20**	**21**
Ford married Betty, 1948	Wilson's daughter, Eleanor, born 1889	Garfield's son, James, born 1865	Barack and Michelle Obama married 1992	Carter's daughter, Amy, born 1967	Hoover died 1964 Benjamin Harrison married Caroline, 1853	Reagan's daughter, Patricia, born 1952
22	**23**	**24**	**25**	**26**	**27**	**28**
Bush's son, Marvin, born 1956			John Adams married Abigail, 1764 Arthur married Ellen, 1859 Frist Lady Caroline Harrison died, 1892	William Henry Harrison's son, Carter, born 1811	Theodore Roosevelt born 1858 Theodore Roosevelt married Alice, 1880	William Henry Harrison's son, John, born 1798
29	**30**	**31**				
	John Adams born 1735 Ivanka Trump born 1981					

NOVEMBER

1	2	3	4	5	6	7
	Polk born 1795 Harding born 1865	Jefferson's daughter, Lucy, born 1780	Lincoln married Mary, 1842	George W. Bush married Laura, 1977		
8	**9**	**10**	**11**	**12**	**13**	**14**
		Peirce married Jane, 1834	Garfield married Lucretia, 1858			
15	**16**	**17**	**18**	**19**	**20**	**21**
		L.B. Johnson married Lady Bird, 1934	Arthur died, 1886	Garfield born 1831	Joe Biden born 1942	Garfield's son, Abra, born 1872
22	**23**	**24**	**25**	**26**	**27**	**28**
Kennedy shot, 1963 Kennedy died, 1963 L.B. Johnson sworn in, 1963	Pierce born 1804	Taylor born 1784	William Henry Harrison married Anna, 1795 Kennedy's son, JFK Jr., born 1960 G.W. Bush's twin daughters Barbara and Jenna, born 1981		Van Buren's son, Abraham, born 1807 Kennedy's daughter, Caroline, born 1957	
29	**30**					
	GHW Bush died 2018					

DECEMBER

1	2	3	4	5	6	7
	Theodore Roosevelt married Edith, 1886			Van Buren born 1782	Tyler's son, Tazewell, born 1830	
8	9	10	11	12	13	14
		Arthur's son, William, born 1860				Washington died 1799
15	16	17	18	19	20	21
			Wilson married Edith, 1915		Van Buren's son, Martin, born 1812	Lincoln's son, William, born 1850
22	23	24	25	26	27	28
	F.D. Roosevelt's son, James, born 1907		Tyler's daughter, Julia, born 1849	Ford died 2006 Truman died 1972		Wilson born 1856 Edith Wilson died 1961
29	30	31				
Andrew Johnson born 1808 Jimmy Carter died 2024	Hayes married Lucy, 1852	Hayes celebrated Silver Anniversary in White House, 1877 Don Trump Jr. born 1977				

TIME LINE

Washington
4/30/1789 – 3/3/1797

Adams
3/4/1797 – 3/3/1801

Jefferson
3/4/1801 – 3/3/1809

Maddison
3/4/1809 – 3/3/1817

Monroe
3/4/1817 – 3/3/1825

J. Q. Adams
3/4/1825 – 3/3/1829

W.H. Harrison
3/4/1841 – 4/4/1841

Jackson
3/4/1829 – 3/3/1837

Van Buren
3/4/1837 – 3/3/1841

Tyler
4/6/1841 – 3/3/1845

Polk
3/4/1845 – 3/3/1849

Taylor

Fillmore
7/10/1850-3/3/1853

Pierce
3/4/1853 – 3/3/1857

Buchanan
3/4/1857 – 3/3/1861

Lincoln
3/4/1861-4/15/1865

A. Johnson
4/15/1865-3/3/1869

3/4/1849-7/9/1850

Garfield
3/4/1881 - 9/19/1881

Grant
3/4/1869 – 3/3/1877

Hayes
3/4/1877 – 3/3/1881

Arthur
9/20/1881 – 3/3/1885

Cleveland
3/4/1885 – 3/3/1889

B. Harrison
3/4/1889 – 3/3/1893

Cleveland
3/4/1893 – 3/3/1897

McKinley
3/4/1897 – 9/14/1901

T. Roosevelt
9/14/1901 – 3/3/1909

Taft
3/4/1909 – 3/3/1913

Wilson
3/4/1913 – 3/3/1921

Harding
3/4/1921 – 8/2/1923

Coolidge
8/3/1923 – 3/3/1929

Hoover
3/4/1929 – 3/3/1933

F. D. Roosevelt
3/4/1933 – 4/12/1945

Truman
4/12/1945 – 1/20/1953

Eisenhower
1/20/1953 – 1/20/1961

Kennedy
1/20/1961 – 11/22/1963

L. B. Johnson
11/22/1963 – 1/20/1969

Nixon
1/20/1969 – 8/9/1974

Ford
8/9/1974 – 1/20/1977

Carter
1/20/1977 – 1/20/1981

Reagan
1/20/1981–1/20/1989

Bush
1/20/1989–1/20/1993

Clinton
1/20/1993–1/20/2001

George W. Bush
1/20/2001–1/20/2009

Obama
1/20/2009–1/20/2017

Donald Trump
1/20/2017–1/20/2021

Joe Biden
1/20/2021–1/20/2025

Donald Trump
1/20/2025–Present

105

Level I

1. George Washington

2. Franklin D. Roosevelt

3. John Fitzgerald Kennedy

4. Abraham Lincoln

5. Franklin D. Roosevelt

6. Abraham Lincoln.

7. Lyndon B. Johnson

8. Franklin D. Roosevelt and, for a couple months, Harry S Truman

9. Ulysses S. Grant

10. Andrew Johnson and William Jefferson Clinton

11.2000

12. Hillary Rodham Clinton

13.Clinton and George W. Bush

14.January 19, 2001, President Clinton's final full day of office

Level II

1. John Adams and Thomas Jefferson

2. William Henry Harrison

3. John Adams-John Quincy Adams and George Bush - George W. Bush

4. George Washington, George Bush, and George W. Bush

5. Harrison; his father was William Henry Harrison, his son was Benjamin Harrison

6. Thomas Jefferson

7. Thomas Jefferson

8. Eight: William Henry Harrison; Zachary Taylor; Abraham Lincoln; James Garfield; William McKinley; Warren Harding; Franklin D. Roosevelt; John F. Kennedy

9. Lyndon B. Johnson and Richard Nixon

10. George Washington and Thomas Jefferson. Martha Washington was the first First Lady. Martha Jefferson was not a First Lady, because she died before Jefferson became president.

11. James Buchanan

12. Jimmy Carter

13. Jimmy Carter

14. Abraham Lincoln

15. Grover Cleveland; when it rang, he answered it himself.

Level III

1. S stands only for S and is written without a period after it. Harry was named after both grandfathers, Solomon and Shippo.
2. James Garfield
3. Franklin D. Roosevelt and Franklin Pierce
4. Grover Cleveland and James Buchanan
5. James Buchanan
6. William Howard Taft, who was 6' 2" and weighed over 300 pounds.
7. James Madison, 5 feet, 100 pounds
8. Taft
9. Dwigh David Eisenhower
10. John Adams, Thomas Jefferson, James Monroe
11. William Henry Harrison
12. Theodore Roosevelt
13. John Fitzgerald Kennedy
14. Woodrow Wilson
15. Dwight David Eisenhower
16. George Bush
17. Joe Biden or Donald Trump
18. Theodore Roosevelt
19. Theodore Roosevelt
20. Thomas Jefferson - George Washington and John Adams bowed to their callers, as was the British custom at the time.

Level IV

1. 1810s. Note: No president yet elected was born in the 1930s, but it is possible to still happen..

2. John Quincy Adams and Andrew Jackson

3. Ulysses S. Grant and Rutherford B. Hayes

4. Richard Nixon and Gerald Ford

5. James Earl Carter and George H.W. Bush

6. 17; plus W. H. Harrison was governor of Indiana Territory, not then a state

7. George Washington

8. James Monroe: Mississippi 1817 Illinois 1818 Alabama 1819 Maine 1820 Missouri 1821

9. Birchard

10. Tyler and Theodore Roosevelt

11. John Fitzgerald Kennedy 11-22-63 Lyndon B. Johnson 1-22-73 Richard Nixon 4-22-94

12. George Washington: Vermont 1791 Kentucky 1792 Tennessee 1796

13. John Tyler had 15 children, eight with first wife Letitia, and seven with his second wife Julia 14. Gerald Rudolph Ford was born Leslie Lynch King, Jr. William Jefferson Clinton waS born William Jefferson Blythe IV.

15. Taft; both were admitted in 1912

16. Ronald Reagan

17. Bess Truman

18. Nine - Eisenhower, Kennedy, Nixon, Carter, Reagan, Bush, Clinton, G.W. Bush, and Obama 19. Frances Cleveland, age 21

20. Theodore Roosevelt, Thomas Jefferson, George Washington, Abraham li ncon

Level V

1. Stephen Grover Cleveland

2. John Quincy Adams, Andrew Johnson

3. Ohio, in 1803

4. Pierce

5. Millard Fillmore, in 1850

6. Monroe, Andrew Johnson, Truman, Ford

7. Andrew Johnson

8. Theodore Roosevelt or Jimmy Carter

9. Eleanor Roosevelt and Eleanor Rosalyn Carter

10. John Adams; John Quincy Adams; John Tyler; John Calvin Coolidge; . John Kennedy

11. Thomas Jefferson; Thomas Woodrow Wilson

12. William Henry Harrison; William McKinley; William Howard Taft; William Clinton

13. Abraham Lincoln

14. Cleveland and Buchanan

15. Van Buren

16. Tyler had 7 children after he left the White House. Cleveland had one child between his 2 terms and 2 children after his second term. Benjamin Harrison had one daughter after he left the White House.

17. Van Buren; the eight previous were born before 1776 in the English Colonies.

18. The first U.S. Census in 1790 covered 13 states and was just under 4 million.

19. James Madison; his predecessors wore knickers.

20. President Taylor's daughter, Sarah Taylor, married Jefferson Davis.

Level VI

1. Wilson, Eisenhower, and Reagan

2. Jefferson, Madison, Monroe, Jackson, Grant

3. 1800s; 1810s: 1950s; 1980s

4. Washington, Jefferson, Madison, Monroe, William Henry Harrison, Tyler, Taylor, Wilson

5. Grant, Hayes, Garfield, Benjamin Harrison, McKinley, Taft, Harding 6. Cleveland

8. Adams, Jefferson, Monroe, Jackson, Van Buren, Tyler, Fillmore, Pierce, Hayes, Arthur, Benjamin Harrison, Theodore Roosevelt, Wilson, Hoover, Nixon

9. Madison, Cleveland, Reagan (second marriage)

10. Tyler

11. Garfield

12. Lyndon B. Johnson

13. Nixon

14. Madison, Monroe, Polk, Buchanan, Garfield, Carter

15. No one. William Henry Harrison died on 4-4-1841 and John Tyler could not be notified and take office until 4-6-1841.

16. Four presidents have entered the executive office in April. They were Tyler, Andrew Johnson, Truman, and George Washington for his first term on 4-3

17. Fillmore, on 7-10-1850 and Lyndon B. Johnson on 11-22-1963.

18. Coolidge, Ford

19. Arthur, Theodore Roosevelt

20. Van Buren, Cleveland, Theodore Roosevelt, Franklin D. Roosevelt

21. Tyler, Benjamin Harrison, Wilson

22. Martha Jefferson, Rachel Jackson, Hannah Van Buren, Ellen Arthur, Alice Roosevelt, Jane Reagan

23. Washington, Madison, Jackson, Polk, Buchanan, Harding

24. Benjamin Harrison: N. Dakota, S. Dakota, Montana, Washington - 1889 Idaho, Wyoming - 1890

25. Washington, William Henry Harrison, Lincoln, Reagan

26. Bush

27. It's not Abigail Van Buren. It's John Adams and Millard Fillmore.

28. Madison

29. Polk

30. McKinley

31. Truman and Eisenhower

32. Bush

33. Fillmore, McKinley, Franklin D. Roosevelt, Nixon

34. Thomas Jefferson George Washington's father died on April 12, 1743 in Virginia.

35. Coolidge

36. Benjamin Harrison, Hoover, Lyndon B. Johnson, Clinton, Obama

37. Taft

38. Hayes

39. Tyler

40. Theodore Roosevelt and Wilson

41. Jackson

42. Theodore Roosevelt

43. James Madison, at age 43 Abraham Lincoln, at age 33 Andrew Johnson, at age 18 Grover Cleveland, at age 49 Calvin Coolidge, at age 33 Harry S Truman, at age 35 John Fitzgerald Kennedy, at age 36 Gerald Ford, at age 35 George W. Bush, at age 31

44. May

45. Van Buren 7-24; Andrew Johnson 7-31; Ulysses S. Grant 7-23
46. Cleveland

47. Washington 12-14; Jefferson 7-4; Adams 7-4; Monroe 7-4; Madison 6-28; Harrison 4-4; Jackson 6-8; Van Buren 7-24; Pierce 10-8; Fillmore 3- 8; McKinley 9-14; Cleveland 6-24; Franklin D. Roosevelt 4-12; Hoover 10-20; Eisenhower 3-28.

48. South Carolina - Jackson New Hampshire - Pierce Pennsylvania - Buchanan Kentucky Lincoln New Jersey - Cleveland Iowa - Hoover Mississippi - Truman California - Nixon Nebraska - Ford Georgia - Carter Illinois Reagan Arkansas - Clinton Connecticut - George W. Bush

49. Polk, Andrew Johnson

50. Arthur, Coolidge

51. Eisenhower, Lyndon B. Johnson

52. Fillmore, McKinley (both died in infancy), Coolidge, Hoover, Eisenhower, Lyndon Johnson, Nixon, and George W. Bush.

53. Truman and Clinton

54. Monroe, Tyler, Pierce, Roosevelt, Roosevelt, Kennedy, Bush

55. Tyler

56. Taylor

57. Lucy Hayes

58. Garfield

59. Ronald Wilson Reagan, William Jefferson Clinton

60. Taylor

BIBLIOGRAPHY

First Ladies, Margaret Truman, Random House, NY 1995

The White House and Its 35 Families, Amy La Follette Jensen, 1970, McGraw-Hill, NY

Facts About the Presidents From George Washington to George Bush, Joseph Nathan Kane, HW Wilson Co., NY, 1989

The Complete Book of U.S. Presidents, William A. DeGregorio, Dembnerbrook, NY, 1984

The First Ladies, Margaret Brown Klapthor, White House Historical Association in Cooperation with National Geographic Society, Washington DC, 1989

The Presidents, First Ladies, and Vice Presidents - White House Biographies 1789-1989, Daniel C. Diller & Stephen L. Robertson, 1989, Congressional Quarterly Inc., Washington, DC

The Buck Stops Here - The Presidents of the United States, Alice Provenson, Harper Trophy a Division of Harper Collins Publishers, 1990

Presidential Wit and Wisdom, Jeff Brallier & Sally Chabert, Penguin Books, 1996

Young Readers Book of Presidents, Wonder Books, 1956, Wonder Books, Phoebe Wilson

The Founding Presidents, edited by Carter Smith, the Millbrook Press, Brookfield, CT, 1993

Presidents of a Young Republic, edited by Carter Smith, the Millbrook Press, Brookfield, CT, 1993

Presidents of a Divided Nation, edited by Carter Smith, the Millbrook Press, Brookfield, CT, 1993

Presidents of a Growing Country, edited by Carter Smith, the Millbrook Press, Brookfield, CT, 1993

Presidents of a World Power, edited by Carter Smith, the Millbrook Press, Brookfield, CT, 1993

Presidents in a Time of Change, edited by Carter Smith, the Millbrook Press, Brookfield, CT, 1993

The Complete Book of American Trivia by Jay Hyams & Kathy Smith, Rutledge Books, New York, 1983